P9-BYN-706

● Read each sentence. Decide which word below belongs in the sentence. Circle that word.

1. Let's go fishing in the ____ .

   stream   stem   sprout

2. The animals are in the ____ .

   barn   burn   born

3. Please bring me some red ____ .

   spread   thread   third

4. Put this ____ on your bed.

   square   quack   quilt

5. Our dog likes to hide her ____ .

   stone   bonnet   bone

6. These ____ fly south in the fall.

   graze   geese   germs

7. Tie the box up with ____ .

   cord   court   clouds

Review: Reading New Words
Preintroduce the following new word that appears in the directions: *circle*.

DISCOVERIES

Houghton Mifflin Reading, 1989 Edition

1

1

- ⭘ change
- ⭘ close
- ⭘ choose

- ⭘ between
- ⭘ below
- ⭘ butter

- ⭘ mine
- ⭘ minute
- ⭘ might

- ⭘ few
- ⭘ feet
- ⭘ fresh

2

- ⭘ throw
- ⭘ though
- ⭘ those

- ⭘ end
- ⭘ egg
- ⭘ engine

- ⭘ south
- ⭘ special
- ⭘ space

- ⭘ instead
- ⭘ instrument
- ⭘ step

3

- ⭘ poor
- ⭘ point
- ⭘ plane

- ⭘ sea
- ⭘ sun
- ⭘ seem

- ⭘ else
- ⭘ east
- ⭘ easy

- ⭘ until
- ⭘ village
- ⭘ usually

4

- ⭘ because
- ⭘ behind
- ⭘ began

- ⭘ land
- ⭘ lion
- ⭘ large

- ⭘ course
- ⭘ corner
- ⭘ cost

- ⭘ floor
- ⭘ fit
- ⭘ fire

Review: Vocabulary Test

Find the number 1. Look at the words in the first box. Find the word *choose*. Mark the space for the word. (Continue in this manner, pronouncing the words to be tested.)

DISCOVERIES

Houghton Mifflin Reading, 1989 Edition

● Read each pair of words. Then read the sentence to the right. Decide which word makes sense in the sentence. Print that word in the sentence.

1. copy
   cowboy

   The _____ will herd the animals past the fence.

2. wheelchair
   whistled

   Richard _____ a happy song as he worked.

3. offered
   often

   Anita _____ to play her harmonica for us.

4. ambulance
   alphabet

   An _____ takes sick people to the hospital.

5. circling
   spelling

   Birds were _____ in the sky above the cornfield.

6. trade
   travel

   Would you _____ your prize for mine?

7. ride
   rust

   Your bicycle will _____ if left out in the rain.

● Think about "A Special Trade."
Read each question. Underline the answer.

1. When Nelly was very small, what did
   Bartholomew do?
   a. He took her for walks in her stroller.
   b. He showed her how to draw pictures.
   c. He stayed away as much as he could.

2. What did Bartholomew do at the sprinkler?
   a. He pushed the stroller around it.
   b. He told Mrs. Pringle to turn it off.
   c. He pushed the stroller quickly through it.

3. Why were they called "ham and eggs"?
   a. Nelly and Bartholomew were always together.
   b. Nelly and Bartholomew liked those foods.
   c. Nelly was small, but Bartholomew was big.

4. What did Nelly do when Bartholomew came
   home from the hospital in a wheelchair?
   a. She told him that their walks were over.
   b. She took him for walks.
   c. She made him a get-well card.

5. What trade did Nelly and Bartholomew make?
   a. They wrote letters to each other.
   b. They helped each other when help was needed.
   c. They gave each other their favorite books.

Comprehension: "A Special Trade"   DISCOVERIES

Houghton Mifflin Reading, 1989 Edition

● Read the story and the questions.
Print the answer to each question.

Claudia and David went to the library with their mother. On a shelf, they saw some little dinosaurs. The librarian told them the dinosaurs' names. Then she showed a movie about how these animals lived and what they ate.

After the movie, Claudia found a book about dinosaurs. The librarian said she could read it at home. David took a book home, too. The children wanted to go back to the library soon.

1. Where did Claudia and David go? _____

2. What was the movie about? _____

3. Who took books home to read? _____

● Listen for the number of syllables
in each of these words. Write the number
on the line after each word.

library _____	shelf _____	book _____
showed _____	movie _____	animals _____
dinosaurs _____	wanted _____	soon _____

Decoding: Hearing Syllables   DISCOVERIES

● Read each sentence. Look at the word in heavy black letters. Print the common syllable or syllables on the line.

1. We need **forty** more blocks to finish our playhouse.

_____

2. The children smiled **sweetly** at me, and I felt happier.

_____

3. The **foundation** of the house isn't finished yet.

_____

4. Ed got an **invitation** to come to Pat's birthday breakfast.

_____

5. The book about flying fish had a **colorful** cover.

_____

6. Gramps very **skillfully** painted a picture of me!

_____

● Now read these questions about the first three sentences. Print your answers.

1. How many more blocks are needed? _____

2. How did the children smile? _____

3. What part of the house isn't finished? _____

Decoding: Common Syllables _ty, tion, ful, ly_

DISCOVERIES

Houghton Mifflin Reading, 1989 Edition

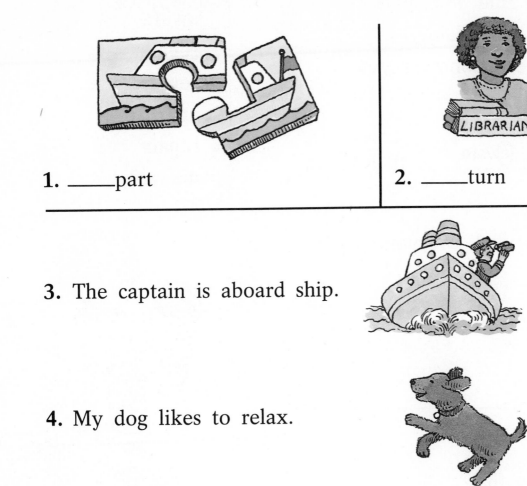

1. ____part

2. ____turn

3. The captain is aboard ship.

4. My dog likes to relax.

5. It is late, and I'll soon be _____ .

        redo   abed

6. Only two eggs _____ .

      remain   ahead

Decoding: Common Beginning Syllables *a, re*

• Finish each sentence with a word from the box. Then find and circle the common beginning syllable. The first one has been done for you.

| ashore |
| aware |
| repaint |
| rewrite |
| apart |
| repair |
| amaze |

1. Bob was not _____(a)ware_____ that his dog was lost.

2. Once the boat landed, everyone went _____ .

3. Mother or Father will _____ the broken train.

4. We will have to _____ one wall of the room.

5. It's easier to take that _____ than it is to put it back together!

6. Didn't the clown's tricks _____ you?

7. I will _____ the letter.

★ Read each word. Find the one that begins with the same common syllable as **rewire**. Mark the space for the answer.

◯ robot   ◯ return   ◯ rattle

Decoding: Common Beginning Syllables *a, re*

DISCOVERIES

Houghton Mifflin Reading, 1989 Edition

● Read each sentence and the words below it. Circle the word that belongs in the sentence. Then print that word in the sentence.

1. A _____ you might like is teaching.

country   career   circling

2. After high school, I'll go to _____ .

color   carrot   college

3. A person who has grown up is an _____ .

against   adult   added

4. Gramps will _____ from his job soon.

radish   rider   retire

5. I want to _____ my acting skills.

develop   detective   doorstep

6. What do you do to _____ for class?

parade   porch   prepare

● What career would you like to have when you grow up? Print a sentence that tells.

_____

• Think about "Growing and Changing."
Read each question. Print the answer.

1. What do all living things do?

_____

_____

2. What are two things you can do now
that you couldn't do as a baby?

_____

_____

3. What are two things you are just
learning to do now?

_____

_____

4. After high school, what do teenagers do?

_____

_____

5. How do adults change?

_____

_____

6. What may people do when they retire?

_____

_____

Comprehension: "Growing and Changing"

DISCOVERIES

Houghton Mifflin Reading, 1989 Edition

● Read each sentence. Decide which
of the two words in the box you would use
to complete the sentence. Print that word
in the sentence.

1. Let's _____ these pages
   into a book.

   | bind |
   | bright |

2. At the mill, workers _____
   the wheat into flour.

   | sigh |
   | grind |

3. The captain of the plane told us
   about our _____ path.

   | fight |
   | flight |

4. The baby's _____ was caused
   by a sudden, loud noise.

   | fright |
   | fight |

5. Your _____ is the upper part
   of your leg.

   | slight |
   | thigh |

6. May I _____ you not to forget
   your house key?

   | rebind |
   | remind |

Decoding/Phonics: Sound Associations for *ind, ight*   DISCOVERIES

● Read each letter. Then answer the questions.

Dear Lost and Found:

  I lost a pretty red umbrella
in your store last Wednesday.
The umbrella was given to me
by a friend for my birthday,
and I miss it! Also, I am going
on a trip soon, and I want
to take the umbrella with me.
Please call me if you have
my umbrella.

Barbara

Dear Lost and Found:

  I lost a ring of five keys
in your store yesterday.
The ring itself is blue, and
two of the keys are gold
in color. On the ring, there
is also a picture of me
with my dog. If you find
the key ring, please call me.
My number is 887-9876.

Carl Fields

1. Which person gave "Lost and Found"

    more help in finding what was lost? _____

2. Who forgot to give a last name

    or a number to call? _____

3. How many keys are on the ring Carl lost? _____

4. What color is the umbrella Barbara lost? _____

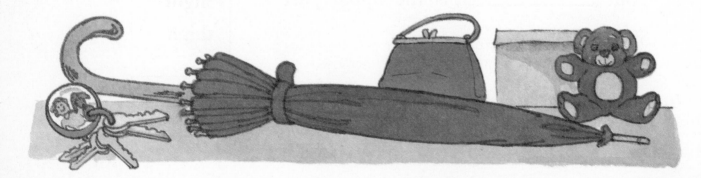

Comprehension: Noting Important Details

DISCOVERIES

Houghton Mifflin Reading, 1989 Edition

● Decide what each group of things is used for. Then print a heading for each group. Choose from the headings in the box.

| Materials for Painting | Materials for Gardening |
| Materials for Sewing | Materials for Building Things |

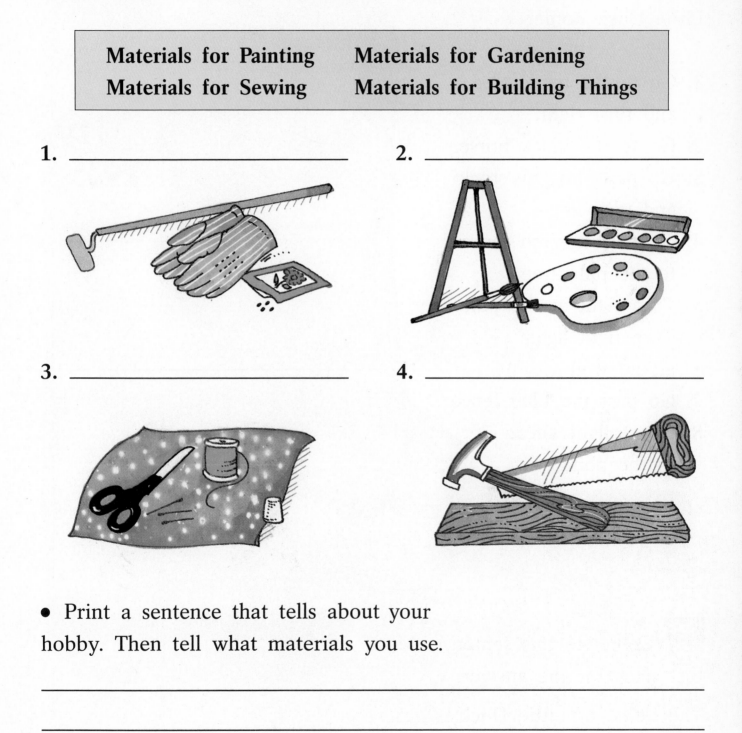

1. _____

2. _____

3. _____

4. _____

● Print a sentence that tells about your hobby. Then tell what materials you use.

_____

_____

_____

• Little Duck is lost again.
Read the directions. Draw a line
along the path that will take
Little Duck home.

1. Go to the apple tree
   and turn right.
2. Go to the black horse.
3. Go past the gray rock
   and turn left.
4. Go past the red fence
   to the pine tree.
5. Turn right at the pine.
6. Turn right again
   at the well.
7. Go past the blue fence.
8. Go straight ahead
   to the pond.

Cattail
Pond

Picnic
Pond

Catfish River

Sunshine Pond

★ Complete this sentence. Mark
the space for the answer.

The home of Little Duck is _____ .

◯ Picnic Pond   ◯ Cattail Pond   ◯ Sunshine Pond

Comprehension: Following Directions
Preintroduce the following new word that appears in the directions: *along*.

DISCOVERIES

Houghton Mifflin Reading, 1989 Edition

● Underline the compound word in each sentence. Draw a line between the two base words in the compound word. Then circle the picture that shows the compound word.

1. Clean your toothbrush well after you brush your teeth.

2. Beth went to the bookstore to get a new book.

3. The children sat around the campfire to keep warm.

● Read each question. The words in heavy black letters can make a compound word that answers the question. Print the answer.

1. What is a **bowl** for a **fish?**

_____

2. What is a **place** for a **fire?**

_____

3. What is a **coat** that you can wear out in the **rain?**

_____

1

○ straight ○ complete ○ yellow ○ direction
○ strong ○ country ○ your ○ during
○ string ○ cleaned ○ young ○ drive

2

○ size ○ catch ○ dry ○ village
○ summer ○ circle ○ drop ○ vowel
○ since ○ class ○ dog ○ visit

3

○ trade ○ start ○ interest ○ life
○ town ○ strong ○ against ○ low
○ trouble ○ stood ○ across ○ later

4

○ lot ○ raise ○ speak ○ surprise
○ loud ○ rail ○ space ○ spelling
○ land ○ right ○ sky ○ suppose

5

○ high ○ year ○ country ○ minute
○ hunt ○ yet ○ course ○ mark
○ hair ○ yard ○ corner ○ material

Vocabulary Test

Find number 1. Look at the words in the first box. Find the word *strong*. Mark the space for the word. (Continue in this manner, pronouncing the words to be tested.)

DISCOVERIES

Houghton Mifflin Reading, 1989 Edition

1.

_____onogra_____

_____

2. Is the **telephone** ringing?

3. Please talk into the **microphone**.

4. Mrs. Cox will make a _____ .

　　　　planter　　　photocopy

5. Jed will take a _____ of us.

　　　photograph　　　paragraph

● Read each paragraph. Circle the picture that goes with it.

1. A **pheasant** is a kind of bird. It is large, with a long tail. Some pheasants are very colorful. Pheasants are often hunted as game.

2. There are many different kinds of **phones** today. Some have buttons you push. Some have no wires at all, so you can use them outdoors. And how do you use a phone? You use it to talk with people, of course!

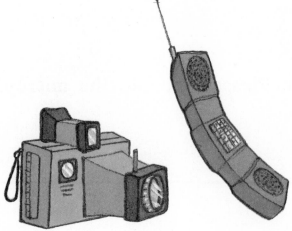

★ Read the sentence. Mark the space for the word you would use to complete it.

Shall we play some music on the _____ ?

○ hamburger

○ microphone

○ phonograph

Decoding/Phonics: Digraph *ph*
Preintroduce the following new word that appears in the directions: *paragraph.*

DISCOVERIES

Houghton Mifflin Reading, 1989 Edition

1. swi____

2. tru____

3. You can **hang** things here.

4. Carol gave me a **wink**.

5. The door closed with a _____ .

   bang   bank

6. The little boat has _____ !

   sung   sunk

Decoding/Phonics: End Sounds *ng, nk*

• Read each sentence. Decide which word below belongs in the sentence and goes with the picture. Circle the word. For the last one, mark the space for the answer.

1. Dan put his money into a ____ .

    bunk   bank   box

2. The bird hurt its ____ .

    foot   swing   wing

3. The book hit the floor with a ____ .

    cook   bang   bring

4. Did that boy ____ at you?

    wink   smile   ink

5. That _____ is black and white.

    zebra   skunk   trunk

★ Watch out for the broken ____ .

  ◯ tent   ◯ lung   ◯ rung

Decoding/Phonics: End Sounds *ng, nk*

DISCOVERIES

Houghton Mifflin Reading, 1989 Edition

● Read each pair of words. Then read the sentence to the right. Decide which word makes sense in the sentence. Print that word in the sentence.

1. camera
   career

   Rita likes to take photographs with her _____ .

2. teenager
   twenty-five

   She has taken _____ pictures of birds.

3. earth
   early

   My brother always awakens _____ in the morning.

4. right
   ring

   If you hear a _____ , someone may be at the door.

5. phone
   microphone

   If the _____ rings, be sure to take a message.

6. parked
   party

   Was your birthday _____ a surprise?

7. announced
   ambulance

   Mr. Long made an announcement, but I didn't hear what he _____ .

● Think about "A Different Day."
Read each group of sentences.
The first sentence tells something that happened.
Underline the sentence below it that tells **why**.

1. Mr. Carr decided to have a party at the zoo.
   a. He was retiring from his job at the zoo.
   b. It was Edgar the Elephant's birthday.

2. The Cortinas were asked to prepare the food.
   a. They made the best Mexican food in town.
   b. They were the only ones who could cook.

3. Ruby and Ricardo got to help their parents.
   a. They always helped on Saturday.
   b. The other workers were sick or on vacation.

4. Mrs. Cortina said the children wouldn't be able
   to see the animals at the zoo.
   a. The animals had been moved to another place.
   b. There was too much work to do for the party.

5. The children got to see many of the animals.
   a. They saw the animals on the way to Edgar's.
   b. Mr. Carr brought the animals into the tent.

6. That night, the children were on the TV news.
   a. They had helped catch a runaway tiger.
   b. They had led the singing of "Happy Birthday."

Comprehension: "A Different Day"　　　　DISCOVERIES

Houghton Mifflin Reading, 1989 Edition

• Look at the words in each box. Circle the common beginning syllable in each word. Then decide which word you would use to complete the sentence. Print that word in the sentence.

1.

| amuse |
| ahead |
| agree |

There was an elephant _____ of me in the parade!

2.

| remove |
| retie |
| repair |

Please _____ your hat when you come inside.

3.

| afraid |
| adore |
| alive |

My little brother is _____ of big dogs.

4.

| relay |
| regret |
| renew |

At this library, you can _____ books for two weeks.

Decoding: Common Beginning Syllables *a, re*

DISCOVERIES

● Read the story. Then number the sentences below from **1** to **4** to show the order in which things happen.

"Mom!" said James. "I can look down at the cornfields!"

James was riding in an airplane for the first time. He thought about all the new things he had seen and done. First, his mother had parked their car in a huge lot. Then they had walked inside to get their tickets.

Once they had their tickets, James and his mother went to a waiting place called a gate. At last, there was an announcement that their plane was ready for boarding.

James had been thinking about this vacation for a long time. But now he didn't want the plane ride to end!

_____ James and his mother board the plane.

_____ James looks out the window at cornfields.

_____ James's mother parks their car in a lot.

_____ James and his mother get their tickets.

Comprehension: Noting Correct Sequence

DISCOVERIES

Houghton Mifflin Reading, 1989 Edition

1.

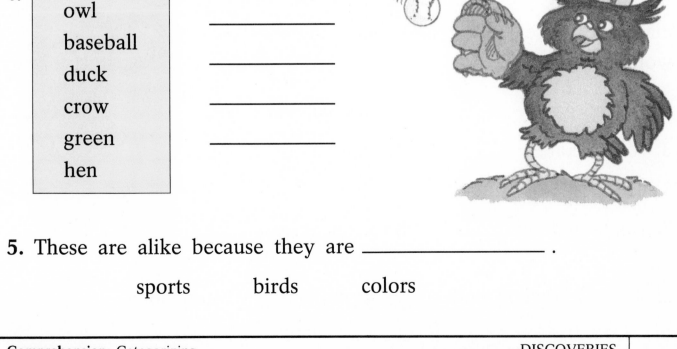

2. These are alike: Wednesday, Saturday.   **Freddy**   **Friday**

3. These are alike: baker, teacher.   **librarian**   **lettuce**

4.

| owl |
| baseball |
| duck |
| crow |
| green |
| hen |

_____

_____

_____

_____

5. These are alike because they are _____ .

sports   birds   colors

Comprehension: Categorizing

Houghton Mifflin Reading, 1989 Edition

● Lisa and Clyde like different things. Read the names of the books that each has read. Then circle the word that tells what each one's hobby is.

Lisa's Books	**Clyde's Books**
Bicycle Racing	*Planting Time*
How to Play Baseball	*Flowers and Vegetables*
Swimming to Win	*How to Grow Cabbage*

Lisa's hobby is ____.	Clyde's hobby is ____.
boating	eating
cars	gardening
sports	stamps

● Now read the words below. If the words name something that would help Lisa, write **L.** If they name something that would help Clyde, write **C.** For the last one, mark the space for the two things that would help Lisa.

1. flower pot ____   2. baseball bat ____

3. roller skates ____   4. plant food ____

5. seeds ____   6. rake ____

7. running shoes ____   8. watering can ____

 ◯ bowling ball ◯ sprinkler ◯ stopwatch

Comprehension: Categorizing

40

● Look at the pictures. Print a sentence
to describe each animal. Use the animal's
name in the sentence.

raccoon   possum

1. _____

_____

2. _____

_____

● Read each sentence and the words below it.
Circle the word that belongs in the sentence.
Then print that word in the sentence.

1. Both raccoons and possums are _____ at night.

active   accident   adult

2. Possums eat small animals and _____ .

instead   innings   insects

3. When an _____ is near, possums stay very still.

empty   enemy   evening

• Think about "Nocturnal Animals."
Look at each picture. Print
the animal's name under its picture.
Then use the names to answer
the questions.

_____ _____ _____

1. Which animal hangs upside down by its tail? _____

2. Which animal can turn its head in almost
   a full circle? _____

3. Which animal rolls over on its back and
   stays very still when an enemy is near? _____

4. Which animal do farmers think of as a friend? _____

5. Which animal do farmers **not** like to have
   in their fields? _____

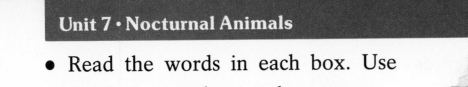

● Read the words in each box. Use a word to complete each sentence. Print the word in the sentence.

cage	stage	hinge	huge

1. Mr. Beat got to do magic tricks on the _____ .

2. Mrs. Rabbit gave a _____ cabbage to her friend.

gym	bridge	giant	badge

3. Frog will go over the _____ in his orange car.

4. The terrible _____ gave us a message.

● Read each sentence again. Find another word that has the same sound for **g** as the word you printed. Print that other word below, next to the number of the sentence.

1. _____   **3.** _____

2. _____   **4.** _____

● Read each pair of sentences.
Underline the word with the **est** ending.
Then circle the picture that answers
the question.

1. All are proud.
Who is the proudest?

2. Two are young.
Which is the youngest?

3. Two are not empty.
Which is the emptiest?

4. Which is the heaviest?
Not all are heavy.

5. Which is the easiest?
One is not easy.

Decoding: Ending *est*

DISCOVERIES

Houghton Mifflin Reading, 1989 Edition

1. thankfully _____   2. saddens _____

_____

3. George is the **sleepiest** one of all.

_____

4. The snow is **hardening** into ice.

_____

_____

5. Yesterday was the _____ day!

        rainiest   roomiest

6. Ronald is _____ the rope.

      tightening   ticketing

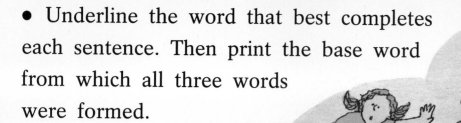

● Underline the word that best completes each sentence. Then print the base word from which all three words were formed.

1. We were ____ a game of ball.
   playing   players   replay

_____

2. Hollie ____ the homework paper.
   finishing   finished   unfinished

_____

3. The kangaroo jumped the ____ of all.
   highly   higher   highest

_____

4. I am even ____ than you are.
   hungriest   hungrier   hungrily

_____

5. Joey ____ Judy at the big game.
   joined   rejoin   joining

_____

★ Find the base word of the word in heavy black letters. Mark the space for the answer.

The lost dog **followed** us home.

◯ follo   ◯ follow   ◯ low

Decoding: Recognizing Base Words
Preintroduce the following new word that appears in the directions: *formed.*

DISCOVERIES

46

Houghton Mifflin Reading, 1989 Edition

● Read each sentence and the words below it.
Circle the word that belongs in the sentence.
Then print that word in the sentence.

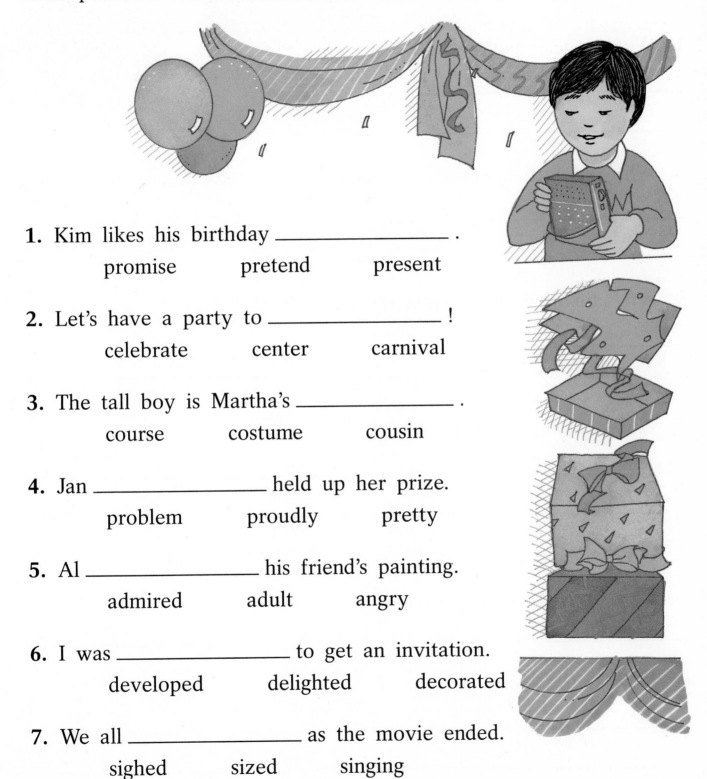

1. Kim likes his birthday _____ .
   promise   pretend   present

2. Let's have a party to _____ !
   celebrate   center   carnival

3. The tall boy is Martha's _____ .
   course   costume   cousin

4. Jan _____ held up her prize.
   problem   proudly   pretty

5. Al _____ his friend's painting.
   admired   adult   angry

6. I was _____ to get an invitation.
   developed   delighted   decorated

7. We all _____ as the movie ended.
   sighed   sized   singing

● Think about "Birthdays."
Read each question.
Print the answer.

1. What special night was it?

_____

_____

2. Why did Little Owl make signs?

_____

_____

3. Why did Little Owl leave the signs by the tree?

_____

_____

4. What did Mole think the signs were?

_____

_____

5. Why did Little Owl let Mole go on thinking that?

_____

_____

6. What is the happy ending of this story?

_____

_____

• Read each pair of sentences.
Decide which word from the box
belongs in each sentence. Print
that word in the sentence.

1. It was a _____ day; the sun

   was out and there were no clouds.

2. Of all the birds I saw at the zoo,

   the _____ was most beautiful.

| pleasant |
| pheasant |

3. You should make a _____

   of your report before handing it in.

4. The _____ is one snake

   that can be dangerous.

| copperhead |
| photocopy |

5. The neighbors may not like it if

   you play the _____ loudly.

6. Jack used a _____

   to carve the wooden figure.

| phonograph |
| pocketknife |

7. Pat's photograph of the team has

   each player's _____ on it.

8. A _____ is a coded message

   that is sent over wires.

| telegraph |
| autograph |

1. they've

they ____ve

2. you're

you ____re

3. We're happy because she's here.

4. They've never seen my dog.

5. She's never been here before.

6. We rested after we'd walked.

We rested after _____ walked.

we had   we would

7. I thought you'd be surprised.

I thought _____ be surprised.

you had   you would

Decoding: Contractions 're, 've, 'd, 's

DISCOVERIES

Houghton Mifflin Reading, 1989 Edition

● Read each sentence and underline the contraction. Write the two words from which the contraction was made.

1. They'd never seen a cow before.   _____ _____

2. I thought they'd like the show.   _____ _____

3. My father doesn't like cats at all.   _____ _____

4. Clara can't baby-sit today.   _____ _____

5. When I find out, I'll let you know.   _____ _____

6. Claude said he's too busy to go with us.   _____ _____

7. This is Alfred. He's come to play ball.   _____ _____

8. Tonight I'm going to the movies.   _____ _____

★ Read each sentence. Look at the words in heavy black letters. Find the contraction that can be made from the words. Mark the space for the answer.

1. **We will** be going to the airport soon.

   ◯ We'd   ◯ We'll   ◯ He'll

2. Mark said **he would** meet us there.

   ◯ he'd   ◯ we'd   ◯ he'll

3. I hope **it is** a big airplane.

   ◯ its   ◯ it's   ◯ it'll

Decoding: Contractions   DISCOVERIES
Preintroduce the following new word that appears in the directions: *contraction*.

Find out what makes a good baseball player.

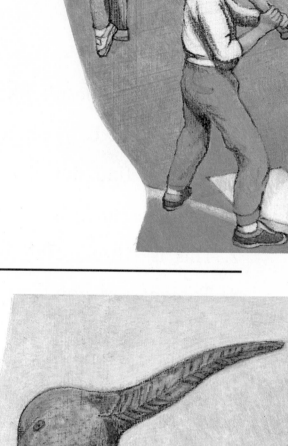

Lots of people like to play baseball. **If you can run fast, you might be good at baseball.** When a baseball player gets a hit, the player runs to the base. **A baseball player must be able to throw a ball far and to catch well.** Baseball is a good game.

A baby frog is called a tadpole. A tadpole doesn't look at all like a grown-up frog. At first, a tadpole has no legs at all. A tadpole has a long tail. It lives in water.

1. A baby frog is called a tadpole. _____

2. A tadpole doesn't look like a grown-up frog. _____

3. At first, a tadpole has no legs at all. _____

4. A tadpole has a long tail. _____

5. A tadpole lives in water. _____

● Read what was said about the winners in this year's dog show. Print the name of each dog under its picture. Then underline the words that helped you decide which dog was which.

1. A prize went to Malka
for her fluffy white coat.
Everyone admired its special cut.
As she was walked around the ring,
Malka looked oh so proud!

_____

2. A prize went to Van Ryan,
even though no one saw his eyes,
which were covered by black fur.
Of all the dogs, Van Ryan was
clearly the most playful.

_____

3. A prize went to Chi-Chi,
the smallest dog in the show.
Her little tail never stopped
wagging, even when the cameras
moved in on her.

_____

★ Read the question.
Mark the space for the answer.

Which dog's fur had a special cut?

◯ Malka's   ◯ Van Ryan's   ◯ Chi-Chi's

Comprehension: Noting Important Details

DISCOVERIES

● Read the questions. Print your answers on the lines. Use the underlined words in your answers. Also use complete sentences.

1. What might you find <u>washed</u> up on a <u>beach</u>?

_____

_____

2. Why is a <u>ferry</u> a good way to get to an <u>island</u>?

_____

_____

3. What kind of <u>weather</u> are dark <u>clouds</u> a sign of?

_____

_____

4. Has the <u>power</u> in your house ever gone out in a <u>storm</u>?

_____

_____

5. When might water around a <u>dock</u> be <u>choppy</u>?

_____

_____

6. Why are <u>seagulls</u> often seen around <u>dunes</u>?

_____

_____

● Think about "Lost in the Storm."
Read each question. Print the
answer. The page number tells
where to find it.

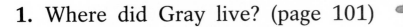

1. Where did Gray live? (page 101)

_____

2. How did Christopher get to Gray's house? (page 102)

_____

3. How did the clouds look as the boys played? (page 103)

_____

4. Why did Christopher stay overnight at Gray's? (page 104)

_____

_____

5. Why was Christopher so upset about Bodger? (page 105)

_____

6. What did Gray's mom think Bodger would do? (page 105)

_____

7. Where did the boys finally find Bodger? (page 110)

_____

_____

● Read each pair of sentences. Find a word in the box to finish each sentence. Print that word in the sentence.

| collie   applied |

1. Pablo's dog is a _____ .
2. Patty _____ the paste with her finger.

| pried   chief |

3. Mom _____ open the can.
4. The farmer's _____ crop is wheat.

| brief   field |

5. Mr. Trent's announcement was _____ and to the point.
6. Everyone laughed when a dog ran out onto the _____ .

● Read about Mr. Toad's problem.
Then follow the directions below.

Mr. Toad has moved into a new house.
He is not happy. The movers have made
a mess of things. Help Mr. Toad get
his house in order. Cross out the thing
that doesn't belong in each box.

1. sofa
   sprinkler
   end table
   easy chair

2. hats
   shirts
   cheese
   slippers

3. pots
   coats
   plates
   mixer

4. hammer
   nails
   tablecloth
   saw

5. crayons
   colored pencils
   finger paints
   crutches

6. bread
   spaghetti
   biscuit mix
   bed

There are four rooms in Mr. Toad's house.
They are listed below. Help Mr. Toad put
the boxes in the right rooms. Write the number
of the box after the room it goes in.

Kitchen _____   Living Room _____

Bedroom _____   Hobby Room _____

● Read each pair of sentences and the words below. Circle the word that belongs in the second sentence. Then print that word in the sentence.

1. Mix red and yellow to make orange.

Red and yellow are _____ colors.

pirate   primary   pretend

2. Olga is going to the library.

She needs _____ for her report.

important   insects   information

3. Tell how the two animals are alike.

In other words, _____ them.

compare   computer   camera

4. Water goes up into the sky and comes back down as rain.

The water _____ always goes on.

bicycle   cycle   crayon

5. Andy can never find his homework papers.

He needs to _____ his things better.

organize   orange   opposite

● Look at this chart. It shows
what the children in Ms. Gray's class
do each morning of the school week.

Ms. Gray's Class—Morning Activities

Time	Monday	Tuesday	Wednesday	Thursday	Friday
9:00	Reading	Reading	Reading	Reading	Reading
10:00	Library	Science	Art	Science	Music
11:00	Spelling	Spelling	Spelling	Spelling	Spelling
11:30	Lunch	Lunch	Lunch	Lunch	Lunch

● Underline the answer to each question.
  For the last one, mark the space for the answer.

1. What do the children do at 9:00 o'clock?
Reading   Science   Spelling

2. On what day do the children have art?
Tuesday   Wednesday   Thursday

3. At what time do the children go to lunch?
  11:00 o'clock   11:30 o'clock   12:00 o'clock

★ How many times a week do the children
have science?

  ◯ 2 times   ◯ 3 times   ◯ 4 times

Reference and Study: Reading Charts   DISCOVERIES

Houghton Mifflin Reading, 1989 Edition

● Read the sentences. Find the one picture that goes with each sentence. Print the word in heavy black letters under the right picture.

1. Annie's arm is in a **sling**.
2. Peter put the boat in the **sink**.
3. Jane likes to play on the **swing**.
4. Would you like a **drink** of this?
5. The **king** was good to his people.
6. Benny sleeps in the top **bunk**.

● Use the words in the box to complete the sentences. Print one word on each line Then print the base word from which all the words in the box were formed.

Base Words

| coloring | colors | colorfully |

1. The houses are _____ painted.

2. How many _____ of paint did they use? _____

3. Jill had fun working in her _____ book.

| shortly | shortened | shortest |

4. Joan _____ her pants so they would fit.

5. Dr. Rosa should be back _____ . _____

6. Which way home is the _____ ?

| sticky | stickers | stickier |

7. Erik put two bumper _____ on his car.

8. The glue makes the paper very _____ . _____

9. The new glue is _____ than the old glue.

1. heaviest

_____

2. overweight

_____ _____

_____

3. Mom put her feet on the footstool.

_____ _____ _____

4. Hal helpfully put away the dishes.

_____

_____

5. Jane looked _____ at the painting.
   admiringly   alphabetically

6. Norma put a _____ cloth on the table.
   patchwork   paintbrush

Decoding: Base Words, Compound Words, Endings

DISCOVERIES

62

● Read each sentence. Use your reading skills
to figure out the word in heavy black letters.
Then underline the answer to each question.
For the last one, mark the space for the answer.

1. The bird is flying **downward**.
   In which direction is downward?
   a. toward the ground   **b.** toward the sky

2. Gramps lived on a farm during his **childhood**.
   When does childhood take place?
   a. when you are old   **b.** when you are young

3. The **nightmare** caused Ted to wake up.
   When might a nightmare happen?
   a. during sleep   **b.** during supper

4. Hank and Kim have a close **friendship**.
   Who can have a friendship?
   a. people who like one another
   b. people who don't get along

Decoding: Base Words, Compound Words, Endings

DISCOVERIES

● Read each pair of words. Then read the sentence to the right. Decide which word makes sense in the sentence. Print that word in the sentence.

1. tornado
   tadpole

   A _____ is a kind of storm.

2. fur
   funnel

   A tornado is like a big _____ of wind.

3. dancing
   damage

   A tornado can do a lot of _____ .

4. thunderstorm
   thousand

   Power may go out during a _____ .

5. area
   arrow

   Last night, a thunderstorm hit our _____ .

6. organizing
   overflowing

   Is there any danger of the river _____ ?

7. voice
   vapor

   Water _____ is made up of tiny bits of water.

● Think about "What Is Weather?"
Read each question.
Underline the answer.

1. What three things work
   together to make weather?
   a. sun   **b.** moon
   c. air   **d.** water

2. As the sun warms the ground and the water,
   what moves into the air?
   a. water vapor   **b.** airplane   **c.** tornadoes

3. What may the water vapor become?
   a. a sunset   **b.** a cloud   **c.** a flood

4. What kind of storm has strong winds that
   move in a shape that looks like a funnel?
   a. a snowstorm   **b.** a thunderstorm   **c.** a tornado

5. How is a rainstorm like a snowstorm?
   a. Both may have strong winds.
   b. Both happen only when it is cold.
   c. Both have drifts that make travel hard.

6. What do weather forecasters do?

   _____

   _____

Comprehension: "What Is Weather?"   DISCOVERIES

● Read each sentence and underline the contraction. Circle the two words from which the contraction was made.

1. Flowers won't grow if they do not get enough sun.

would not   will not   can not

2. Jed got a computer, and it's just what he wanted.

it has   it would   it is

3. Mary said she'd like to play with us.

she would   she had   she is

4. When I grow up, I'm going to be a scientist.

I am   I will   I would

● Read each sentence. Print the contraction for the words in heavy black letters.

1. Roy said **he would** like to stay longer.   _____

2. Ask Kate and Laura if **they will** help.   _____

3. I cannot tell if **it is** still raining.   _____

4. Mrs. Cook **is not** at school today.   _____

Comprehension: Contractions   DISCOVERIES

     Houghton Mifflin Reading, 1989 Edition

• Jed made a chart to show all the things he ate one day. Use the chart to answer the questions below.

Food on Wednesday

Breakfast				
Lunch				
After School				
Supper				

1. What fruit did Jed eat for breakfast? _____

2. What hot food did Jed eat for lunch? _____

3. What two vegetables did Jed eat for supper? _____

4. How many eggs did Jed eat all day? _____

5. How many glasses of milk did Jed have? _____

1.

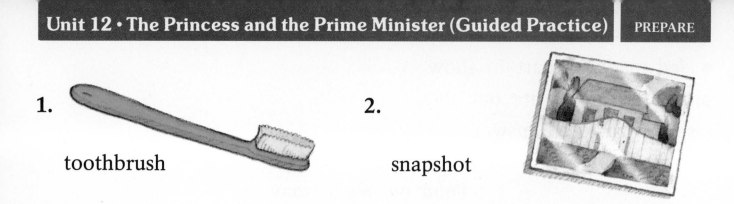

toothbrush

2.

snapshot

3. You can see **smoke** and **flames**.

4. Don't **smash** the **fresh** eggs!

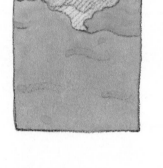

5. Ms. Harvey teaches second _____ now.

          trade   grade

6. If you liked the show, _____ your hands.

          clap   flap

Decoding/Phonics: Consonant Review: Clusters, Digraphs

DISCOVERIES

Houghton Mifflin Reading, 1989 Edition

● Read each sentence. Decide which word below belongs in the sentence and goes with the picture. Print that word in the sentence. For the last one, mark the space for the answer.

1. Mix this with a wooden _____ .

   spoon   stone   prune

2. Did the _____ breathe fire?

   flashlight   dragon   shaggy

3. A _____ is a kind of fruit.

   free   sheriff   cherry

4. Is there gold in that _____ ?

   chest   thirst   crash

5. A _____ is a kind of plant.

   sheepskin   bracelet   mushroom

★ What movie is playing at the ___ ?

   ◯ chatter   ◯ tractor   ◯ theater

Decoding/Phonics: Consonant Review: Clusters, Digraphs

DISCOVERIES

● Read the words in the box.
Use them to complete the story.
Print one word on each line.

castle
princess
mountain
balcony
stream
king
queen
defend

The _____ wanted to build a new home for his family. He drew up plans for a _____ and showed them to the queen. The _____ liked the plans. But she wanted to add a _____ off the main room. So a balcony was added.

The king and queen were happy with the plans. But they argued about where in the kingdom to build their castle. The king wanted to live near a _____ so he could fish every day. The queen wanted to live in the village.

Then their daughter, the _____ , got an idea. "Let's put our castle on top of that _____ ," she said. "Up there, our home will be easy to _____ ."

● Where do you think the castle should be? Print a sentence that tells.

_____

● Think about "The Princess and
the Prime Minister." Read each group of sentences.
Put **1** by the sentence that should be first.
Put **2** by the sentence that should be next.
Put **3** by the sentence that should be last.

1. The Princess announced she would take over. _____

   It was decided that there be a test. _____

   The Prime Minister ruled the Kingdom badly. _____

2. The Messenger went off to find out why. _____

   The mountain stream stopped flowing. _____

   A Dragon was reported to be using the water. _____

3. The Dragon scared the people away. _____

   The Prime Minister led the people to the Dragon. _____

   The Prime Minister told everyone to charge. _____

4. The Princess gave the Dragon a present. _____

   The Princess went off to make something. _____

   The Princess climbed up the mountain. _____

5. The Dragon put on his new shoes. _____

   After that, the Princess ruled the Kingdom. _____

   The Dragon gave back the stream. _____

● Read each sentence. Look carefully at the word in heavy black letters. Print the base word of that word.

1. The game is not **completely** over.

_____

2. The dog wagged its tail **playfully**.

_____

3. Richard was the **proudest** of all!

_____

4. The **rulers** were the king and queen.

_____

5. Those **flashing** lights are a warning.

_____

6. Paula has a **handful** of sand.

_____

7. Beth is **skipping** down the street.

_____

8. Roger is **taping** up our pictures.

_____

Decoding: Recognizing Base Words

DISCOVERIES

Houghton Mifflin Reading, 1989 Edition

● Read each part of the story.
Decide what you think will happen next.
Underline your answer.

1. Ann's grandpa promised to take Ann to a ball game today if it was nice. When Ann got up, it was raining.

a. They will go to the game.

b. They won't go to the game.

2. As Ann was eating breakfast, Mom said, "I think it will stop raining. The sun is starting to come out."

a. They will go to the game.

b. They won't go to the game.

3. Ann's grandpa said, "Oh, no! I forgot. My car's being fixed."

Mom said, "I'm not using my car today."

a. They will take Mom's car.

b. Grandpa will buy a new car.

4. At the park, Ann and Grandpa stopped at a window and gave a man some money. The man gave them two tickets.

a. They will go home.

b. They will go into the ball park.

5. Ann and Grandpa hurried to their seats. Soon after they sat down, they saw the team come onto the playing area.

a. The game will begin.

b. The game will end.

6. Soon after the game began, Ann and Grandpa felt hungry. Grandpa gave Ann some money. Ann left her seat.

a. Ann will go home to dinner.

b. Ann will buy things to eat.

Comprehension: Predicting Outcomes

1. spoke   2. brush   3. gift   4. wade

_____

5. The cat **crept** from under the bed.   long   short

_____

6. The sun **shone** all afternoon.   long   short

_____

7. Did you ever ride on a **mule**?   long   short

_____

_____

8. There is a _____ in Jerry's kite.

rip   ripe

9. Beth likes the _____ blue flowers.

pal   pale

● Read each sentence. Decide which word below belongs in the sentence. Circle that word. For the last one, mark the space for the answer.

1. Let's put the dog into the ____ .

   tub   tube

2. Pick only the ____ fruit.

   rip   ripe

3. Bob has a new yellow ____ .

   rob   robe

4. A ____ is a close friend.

   pal   pale

5. Don't give the dog table ____ .

   scraps   scrapes

6. A red ____ is a vegetable.

   bet   beet

★ Mom will ____ the meat for us.

   ◯ slice   ◯ slick   ◯ sleek

Decoding/Phonics: Long and Short Vowels

DISCOVERIES

1.

late_____

2.

tooth_____

3. He shows his **gladness**.

4. The girl is **hatless**.

5. In winter, the tree is _____ .

    leafless   likeness

6. Look at the _____ of those houses!

    colorless   closeness

Decoding: Common Syllables *less, ness*

● Circle the word that makes sense in each sentence. For the last one, mark the space for the answer.

1. Feel the ____ of the kitten's fur!

    softness   shapeless   smartness

2. I don't like being in a ____ room.

    whiteness   weakness   windowless

3. The woods are scary in the ____ of night.

    darkness   cloudless   loudness

4. Those dogs are known for their ____ with children.

    poorness   powerless   gentleness

5. Jed was tired after such a ____ night.

    sleepless   sleepiness   spotless

6. Sally missed school because of ____ .

    illness   homeless   endless

★ James couldn't carry the box very far because of its ____ .

    ◯ heaviness   ◯ headless   ◯ hopeless

Decoding: Common Syllables *less, ness*   DISCOVERIES

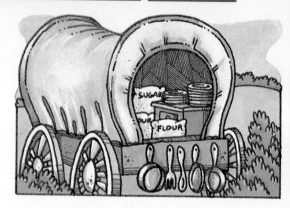

• Read the questions. Print your answers on the lines. Use the underlined words in your answers. Also use complete sentences.

1. What might you find <u>among</u> the things in this covered <u>wagon</u>?

_____

_____

2. If someone is working at a <u>loom</u>, what might the person be <u>weaving</u>?

_____

_____

3. How would a <u>rug</u> made from <u>sheepskin</u> feel? Would it be hard or soft?

_____

_____

4. Why isn't a <u>corral</u> a good place for animals to <u>graze</u>?

_____

_____

5. How are a <u>canyon</u> and a <u>mesa</u> alike? How are they different?

_____

_____

● Think about "Nannabah's Friend."
Read each group of sentences.
The first sentence tells something that happened.
Underline the sentence below it that tells **why.**

1. Nannabah was afraid to go to the canyon.
   a. She had never gone there alone.
   b. She was afraid of the sheep.

2. Nannabah shook a can of rocks at the sheep.
   a. It was a way to wake the sheep up.
   b. It kept the sheep on the trail.

3. The sheep stopped by a pool in the canyon.
   a. They were frightened by a snake.
   b. They wanted to graze on the green grass.

4. Nannabah made two dolls from the red mud.
   a. She didn't like being all alone.
   b. She made them for her grandmother.

5. Nannabah named the dolls "Little Sister" and "Baby Brother."
   a. She wanted a sister or a brother.
   b. They made her think of her own family.

6. The next day, Nannabah was not alone.
   a. Another girl had brought her sheep there.
   b. Grandmother could go with her.

● Read each sentence and the words below it. Circle the word that makes sense and has the same beginning sound or sounds as the picture name.

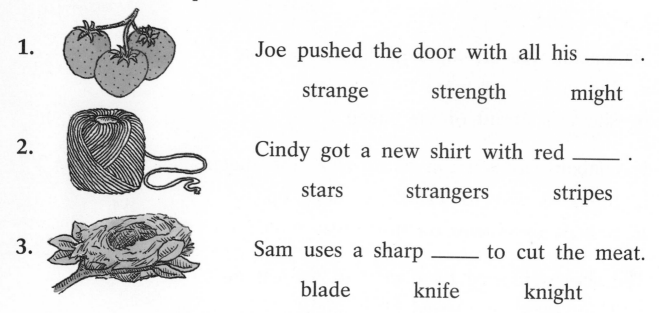

1. Joe pushed the door with all his ____ .

    strange   strength   might

2. Cindy got a new shirt with red ____ .

    stars   strangers   stripes

3. Sam uses a sharp ____ to cut the meat.

    blade   knife   knight

● Now circle the word that makes sense and has the same ending sound or sounds as the picture name.

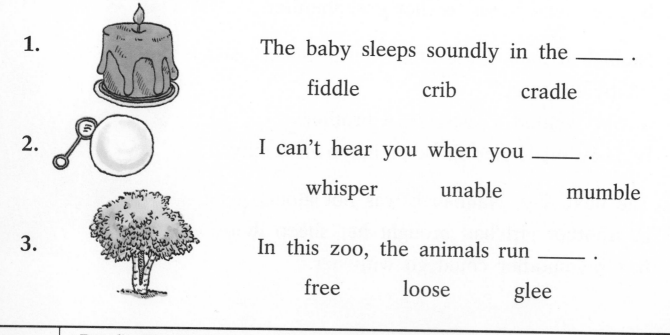

1. The baby sleeps soundly in the ____ .

    fiddle   crib   cradle

2. I can't hear you when you ____ .

    whisper   unable   mumble

3. In this zoo, the animals run ____ .

    free   loose   glee

Decoding/Phonics: Using Letter Sounds and Printed Context

DISCOVERIES

Houghton Mifflin Reading, 1989 Edition

● Read each sentence. The word in heavy black letters is new. Use your reading skills to figure it out. Then underline the answer to each question.

1. Rose was **heartbroken** when her cat was lost. How does a heartbroken person feel?

   a. quite angry   **b.** very sad

2. Peter watered the **overhanging** plant. Where would you look to see such a plant?

   a. up   **b.** down

3. Jasper is the **sleepiest** person in our family. What might the sleepiest person be like?

   a. be more sleepy than others   **b.** not be sleepy

4. The book was **hidden** under the magazine. Where would a hidden book be?

   a. in clear sight   **b.** out of sight

5. I will buy three books from the **shopkeeper.** Where does a shopkeeper work?

   a. in a store   **b.** a ship

• Read the story. Then number the sentences from **1** to **4** to show the order in which things happen.

Baby bears are born in winter. At first, their eyes are closed. Their little bodies have no fur. Their mother keeps the cubs warm.

Four weeks later, the cubs' eyes open. By then, their bodies are covered with soft fur. Still, they stay inside their cave, where it is nice and safe. Their mother feeds them.

When they are about nine weeks old, their mother leads the cubs from the cave. Now it is spring. The baby bears are ready to play!

_____ The baby bears open their eyes.

_____ The baby bears begin to get fur.

_____ The bears leave the cave.

_____ The baby bears are born.

★ When are the cubs ready to play? Mark the space for the answer.

◯ summer   ◯ fall   ◯ winter   ◯ spring

Comprehension: Noting Correct Sequence

DISCOVERIES

Houghton Mifflin Reading, 1989 Edition

● Read the words in the boxcars. Use them to answer the questions. Print one word on each line. Use each word only once.

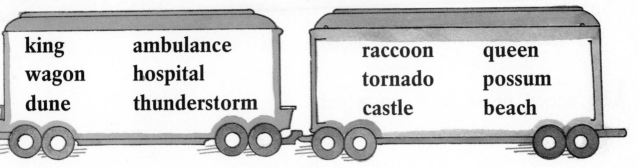

king	ambulance		raccoon	queen
wagon	hospital		tornado	possum
dune	thunderstorm		castle	beach

1. Which two things have wheels?

_____   _____

2. Which two are buildings?

_____   _____

3. Which two are people who rule?

_____   _____

4. Which two are kinds of weather?

_____   _____

5. Which two are made up of sand?

_____   _____

6. Which two are nocturnal animals?

_____   _____

● Choose any pair of words from above. Print a sentence that uses the two words.

_____

_____

● Read each sentence. Decide which of the words in the box you would use to complete the sentence. Print that word in the sentence.

1. The sheep need grass on which to _____ .

| blaze |
| graze |

2. Let's rest in the _____ of that big tree.

| shade |
| grade |

3. We followed the _____ through the woods.

| frail |
| trail |

4. What kind of _____ is that coat made from?

| cloth |
| broth |

5. A kangaroo carries her baby in a _____ .

| post |
| pouch |

6. If we don't _____ , we'll miss the bus!

| rung |
| rush |

7. This is the _____ time I have seen that show.

| thread |
| third |

• Follow these directions.

1. Print the letter **O** so big that it
   takes up most of the space
   at the bottom of this page.
2. Print the letter **U** in the middle
   of the big **O**.
3. Print the letter **V** under the **U**,
   near the bottom of the big **O**.
4. Print two **O**'s in the big **O**. Print
   them in a line above the **U**, one
   on each side of the **U**.
5. Print the letter **S** ten times
   along the outside top of the big **O**.

1

- ○ among
- ○ area
- ○ admire

- ○ cook
- ○ cloud
- ○ correct

- ○ bell
- ○ bright
- ○ build

- ○ kept
- ○ deep
- ○ queen

2

- ○ full
- ○ farm
- ○ fact

- ○ mud
- ○ meat
- ○ mountain

- ○ record
- ○ reach
- ○ rule

- ○ sand
- ○ safe
- ○ star

3

- ○ bag
- ○ bad
- ○ board

- ○ power
- ○ proud
- ○ present

- ○ shape
- ○ snake
- ○ stone

- ○ insect
- ○ lead
- ○ island

4

- ○ study
- ○ center
- ○ sent

- ○ truck
- ○ taste
- ○ thin

- ○ bit
- ○ bottom
- ○ bowl

- ○ princess
- ○ past
- ○ plan

5

- ○ weather
- ○ wagon
- ○ wash

- ○ finger
- ○ king
- ○ wing

- ○ crop
- ○ lay
- ○ early

- ○ noise
- ○ voice
- ○ nest

Vocabulary Test

Find number 1. Look at the words in the first box. Find the word *among*. Mark the space for the word. (Continue in this manner, pronouncing the words to be tested.)

DISCOVERIES

Houghton Mifflin Reading, 1989 Edition

1. s____l

2. s____p

3. b____t

4. w____d

5. Your pail has a **leak** in it.   mean   bread

6. The sun can make you **sweat**.   deal   head

7. This looks like a good _____ .
   meal   mail

8. Rain will _____ this boat.
   soak   seek

● Read all the sentences in Column 1. Use the words in heavy black letters to complete the sentences in Column 2. Print one word in each sentence. For the last one, mark the space for the answer.

Column 1

1. Jim **laid** his schoolbooks on the table.

2. Nancy wants some butter for her **toast.**

3. Will you help me pick some **beans** from the garden?

4. Is there any **mail** for me in the box?

5. There was a lunch on each of the **trays.**

6. Margaret's **cheeks** are red from the cold.

Column 2

_____ is made from bread.

The word _____ means "put down."

Letters and bills are both _____ .

_____ are part of a person's face.

_____ help you to carry things.

★ _____ are a kind of vegetable.

◯ Beans

◯ Cheeks

◯ Trays

Decoding/Phonics: Vowel Pairs Review
Preintroduce the following new word that appears in the directions: *column.*

DISCOVERIES

Houghton Mifflin Reading, 1989 Edition

● Read the questions. Print your answers on the lines. Use complete sentences for your answers.

1. Which is free — a bird in a cage or a bird on the wing?

_____

2. Which is greater — one hundred or one million?

_____

3. Which is a fruit — a strawberry or a cabbage?

_____

4. Which have disappeared from earth — snakes or dinosaurs?

_____

5. Which is easier to find in haystacks — straw or needles?

_____

6. If an animal is hitched, can it run free?

_____

7. Would tangled reins be a problem to a cowboy?

_____

• Think about "One Big Wish."
Read each group of sentences.
Put **1** by the sentence that should be first.
Put **2** by the sentence that should be next.
Put **3** by the sentence that should be last.

1. The woman gave Fred one wish. _____

   Fred freed the woman from the brambles. _____

   Fred wished for all his wishes to come true. _____

2. Dollar bills began to fall from the sky. _____

   Fred wished for a wagon to hold the money. _____

   Fred wished for a million dollars. _____

3. Fred wished for a pair of horses. _____

   Fred wished there were six of him. _____

   All the Freds started talking at once. _____

4. Fred wished the whole thing hadn't happened. _____

   All the Freds wished everything would stop. _____

   Fred found himself back in his field. _____

5. Once again, Fred freed the woman. _____

   Fred wished the woman a good morning. _____

   Once again, the woman gave Fred a wish. _____

Comprehension: "One Big Wish"

DISCOVERIES

Houghton Mifflin Reading, 1989 Edition

● Read each sentence and the pair of words below it. Decide which word belongs in the sentence. Circle that word.

1. The wall is made of ____ .

   brick   brake

2. What is today's ____ ?

   dart   date

3. The shoe needs a ____ .

   sill   sole

4. I'll give the dog a ____ .

   bone   bank

5. Please turn on the ____ .

   lamp   lump

6. Put water in the ____ .

   jug   jig

7. A ____ is a tool.

   wrench   ranch

8. That ____ can kick!

   mail   mule

9. Who ____ that hole?

   dug   dull

10. Here's a ____ of cheese.

    slick   slice

11. Tom lives on that ____ .

    blaze   block

12. This river is ____ .

    wide   wade

13. We took a ____ by car.

    trip   trap

14. Make a ____ with your hand.

    file   fist

Decoding/Phonics: Long and Short Vowels

DISCOVERIES

● Look at the words in each box.
Circle the common syllable
in each word. Choose a word
to complete the sentence. Print
that word in the sentence.

1. | brightness
    | blindness
    | breathless

After riding up the hill, Bart
was _____ .

2. | powerless
    | pointless
    | pageless

Many homes in the village were
_____ after the storm.

3. | happiness
    | hardness
    | heaviness

Harriet showed her _____
by smiling.

4. | lightness
    | lifeless
    | loveliness

From the _____ of the box,
I figured it must be empty.

1. Sparky, my dog is in the wagon.

    a. someone is talking to Sparky

    b. more is being told about Sparky

2. Sparky, my dog, is in the wagon.

    a. someone is talking to Sparky

    b. more is being told about Sparky

3. Dr. Green the scientist is Bill's mother.

4. I saw Mr. Park my teacher at the store.

5. Tom my older brother likes horses.

6. Mr. Lee Katy's father has a computer.

● Read each pair of sentences. Underline the sentence that tells more about someone just named.

1. Felicia, my pet turtle got out of her box.

   Felicia, my pet turtle, got out of her box.

2. Reggie, my brother, took my bicycle.

   Reggie, my brother took my bicycle.

3. Beatrice, my best friend is staying with us.

   Beatrice, my best friend, is staying with us.

4. Ben, my little brother, cries all the time.

   Ben, my little brother cries all the time.

5. Ann, Barbara, and Janet are working hard.

   Ann, Janet's friend, is working hard.

6. Duke, my cat, is sleeping.

   Duke, Andy, and Alfred are sleeping.

★ Read the sentences. Mark the space by the sentence that shows someone is being spoken to.

   ◯ Ira, the baby is sick.

   ◯ Ira, the baby, is sick.

   ◯ Ira is sick.

Bernice jumped on her new bicycle. She rode to her friend Paul's house.

"Look, Paul," she said. "How do you like my new bicycle?"

"It's great!" said Paul. "May I ride it?"

Bernice got off the bicycle. She didn't answer right away. She hadn't had the bicycle for very long. She wanted to ride it herself.

"Please let me try it," said Paul.

Bernice thought about what a good friend Paul was. She knew he took good care of things. "You can ride it," she said.

Bernice and Paul both smiled as Paul rode down the street.

—— The story takes place at Paul's house.

—— Bernice lets Paul ride her bicycle.

—— The story is about Bernice and Paul.

—— Bernice shows Paul her new bicycle.

—— Paul wants to ride the bicycle, but Bernice isn't sure she wants him to.

Reference and Study: Summarizing

• Read this summary of a story you know. Answer the questions. For the last one, mark the space for the answer.

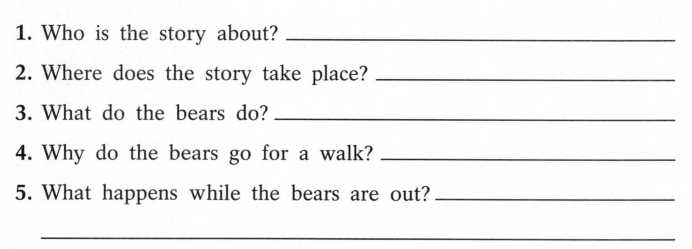

This story is about a girl named Goldilocks and a family of bears. At the start of the story, the bears are at home, sitting down to eat. Since their food is too hot, they go out for a walk. That's when Goldilocks comes along. She eats the food of Baby Bear, breaks his chair, and climbs into his bed. The bears return home and find Goldilocks. She runs away.

1. Who is the story about? _____

2. Where does the story take place? _____

3. What do the bears do? _____

4. Why do the bears go for a walk? _____

5. What happens while the bears are out? _____

_____

★ What important thing happens last?

◯ Goldilocks eats Baby Bear's food.

◯ The bears return and find Goldilocks.

◯ Goldilocks runs away.

Houghton Mifflin Reading, 1989 Edition

• Read each pair of words. Then read the sentence to the right. Decide which word makes sense in the sentence. Print that word in the sentence.

1. explained   Mother _____
   example   why the dog couldn't come in.

2. exactly   That movie was the most
   exciting   _____ one I've seen.

3. station   The train has just arrived
   stone   at the _____.

4. mirror   It's proper that the _____
   mayor   lead the town parade.

5. moment   Maria said, "Wait a _____
   mountain   while I get my coat."

6. eight   You may choose _____ of
   either   the two kittens.

7. slumped   The tired boy _____ back
   slipped   in his chair.

● Think about "Sumi and the Tokyo Express."
Read each question. Print the answer.

1. What had Mr. Oda just gotten?

_____

_____

2. What did Sumi take to the goat?

_____

_____

3. Why was Sumi excited about the goat?

_____

_____

4. What did Ayako tell the class?

_____

_____

5. Why wouldn't the train stop at Sugi Village?

_____

_____

6. Why did the children lose interest in the train?

_____

_____

Comprehension: "Sumi and the Tokyo Express" (Part One)   DISCOVERIES

Houghton Mifflin Reading, 1989 Edition

● Read each riddle below.

Think what the riddle is telling about.

Circle the right answer for the question.

Underline the words in the riddle

that gave you clues.

1. I am something
   That grows in the ground.
   If you like tall green things,
   Then you'll want me around.
   What am I?

   frog   tree   flower

2. I am something
   That lives in a tree.
   When you think of flying,
   You think of me.
   What am I?

   monkey   nest   bird

3. I'm made up of pages
   That are filled with words.
   I'm only for people,
   Not for pets or for birds.
   What am I?

   book   pencil   car

4. I am something
   That lights up the night.
   Just keep me from wind.
   My light will stay bright.
   What am I?

   flower   candle   plant

5. You use me when
   It's time to pound
   A nail in a board
   Or a stick in the ground.
   What am I?

   hammer   saw   rake

6. I am a color
   You might see in the sky
   On days when there's sun,
   Or on days when it's dry.
   What color am I?

   green   blue   black

Comprehension: Drawing Conclusions

Preintroduce the following new word that appears in the directions: *riddle*.

DISCOVERIES

Houghton Mifflin Reading, 1989 Edition

1. Andrea dropped the glass on the floor.

_____ The glass broke.

_____ Andrea wasn't being careful.

2. Gregory couldn't find his hat.

_____ Sally hid Gregory's hat.

_____ Gregory went out to play.

---

3. Alfred was taking care of the baby. Just as the baby fell asleep, the cat came into the room. It jumped on Alfred. He gave a loud shout. **The baby woke up.**

_____ The baby went to sleep.

_____ The cat came into the room.

_____ Alfred gave a loud shout.

4. Every year, trees make new seeds. The seeds fall to the ground. Some land on rock. These seeds will not grow. **Other seeds land in the soft dirt.** These seeds may become new trees.

_____ Trees make seeds every year.

_____ Seeds will not grow on rock.

_____ These seeds may become new trees.

Comprehension: Cause-Effect Relationships

DISCOVERIES

100

● Read each part of the story and the question on the right. Put an **X** by your answer. For the last one, mark the space for the answer.

1. Max jumped onto Pam's bed. He knew he shouldn't be there, but Pam's new blanket was soft and nice.

Why did Max jump on the bed?

_____ He liked to sleep.

_____ He liked the new blanket.

_____ It was Pam's bed.

2. On the bed was a box of Pam's stamps. Max jumped on the box. Soon the stamps were all over the bed.

Why were stamps everywhere?

_____ Max jumped on the box.

_____ Max ate a stamp.

_____ The box had a hole in it.

3. Pam came into the room. Stamps were all over the bed. "Look at all my stamps!" Pam cried. "Max, you shouldn't be on the bed!"

What happened because Pam's stamps were all over her bed?

_____ She was upset.

_____ She laughed.

_____ She ran after Max.

★ Pam gathered the stamps and went to get another box. While she was gone, a wind came in the open window. Once again, there were stamps all over.

What happened because of wind?

◯ Pam closed the window.

◯ Max ran away.

◯ Stamps were everywhere.

Comprehension: Cause-Effect Relationships   DISCOVERIES

● Read the words on the left. Draw a line from each word to the word or word group on the right that means the opposite.

strange   common
silence   in an excited way
famous   not free from
calmly   not known
excused   noise

● Read the words in the box. Decide which word you would use to complete each sentence. Print that word on the line.

conductors	honor	passengers	attention

1. _____ are people who work on trains.

2. _____ are people who pay to ride on trains.

3. We thought it was an _____ to speak to the baseball star.

4. Give the mayor your _____ when she speaks.

● Think about "Sumi and the Tokyo Express."
Read each sentence beginning. Decide which
group of words is the correct ending.
Underline your answer.

1. Sumi was excited about the goat because
   a. she liked the goat's warm milk.
   b. she had something to tell the class.

2. The class soon forgot about the goat because
   a. Ayako had more exciting news to tell.
   b. everyone in Sugi Village had a goat.

3. Sumi called the train unfriendly because
   a. it would never stop at Sugi Village.
   b. it was very old and very ugly.

4. The train stopped at Sugi Village because
   a. train workers saw something on the tracks.
   b. many passengers were waiting at the station.

5. It was good that Miki had a red hat because
   a. she might not have been seen in the snow.
   b. she might have caught a cold.

6. Everyone thought the goat was special because
   a. the goat had stopped the Tokyo Express.
   b. no other goat in the village had a red hat.

• Read each sentence and the words below it.
Circle the word that belongs in the sentence.
Then print that word in the sentence.

1. Soft as feathers, the _____ fell.

snowflakes   downstairs   earthquakes

2. Cindy has a new watch on her _____ .

wrong   wrench   wrist

3. Everyone eats soup with a _____ .

moon   spoon   cool

4. During the spring, cowboys cut the sheep's _____ .

hook   hood   wool

5. The ice is too _____ for skating.

thump   thin   therefore

Decoding/Phonics: Using Letter Sounds and Printed Context   DISCOVERIES

Houghton Mifflin Reading, 1989 Edition

• Read each sentence. Then read the answer choices. Circle the word you would use to complete each sentence.

1. When did you ____ that letter?

    aim   mail   maid

2. There is a full ____ tonight.

    mow   moon   moan

3. Mr. Willis is ____ of the baseball team.

    chair   coach   couch

4. You need red ____ to sew on those buttons.

    treat   teeth   thread

5. The flowers are in ____ now.

    bloom   beat   bleed

6. There are ____ of paint on that wall.

    streaks   sprawls   steaks

7. Mom reads the newspaper ____ .

    doily   dainty   daily

● Read each pair of sentences.
The word in heavy black letters has
more than one meaning. Put the number
of the sentence under the picture that
shows the correct meaning for that word.
For the last sentence, mark the space
for the word's meaning.

1. The man was a shoemaker by **trade**.
2. Sue made a **trade** with Paula.

_____   _____

1. Emma's dog stays in this **pen** at nigh
2. I can write a letter with this **pen**.

_____   _____

1. A pencil has a **point** at one end.
2. **Point** to the right house.

_____   _____

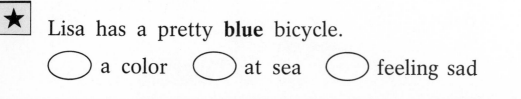
★ Lisa has a pretty **blue** bicycle.

◯ a color   ◯ at sea   ◯ feeling sad

● Choose a word from the box to complete each sentence. Print one letter of the word on each of the small lines. The first one has been done for you.

> context
> million
> moment
> station
> silence
> famous

1. The opposite of **noise** is s (i) l e n c e .

2. If thousands of people know you you're __ __ (o) __ __ __ .

3. A stopping place for trains is a __ __ __ __ __ (o) __ .

4. A number greater than one hundred or one thousand is one __ __ __ __ (o) __ __ .

5. A very short time is a __ __ __ __ __ (o) .

6. If a word is used in (o) __ __ __ __ __ __ it is part of a sentence.

● Read the question. For the answer, finish each word. Use the circled letters above.

What time is it when an elephant sits on a fence?

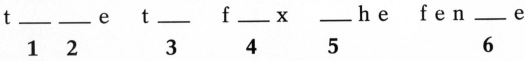

t __ __ e   t __   f __ x   __ h e   f e n __ e
  1 2   3   4   5   6

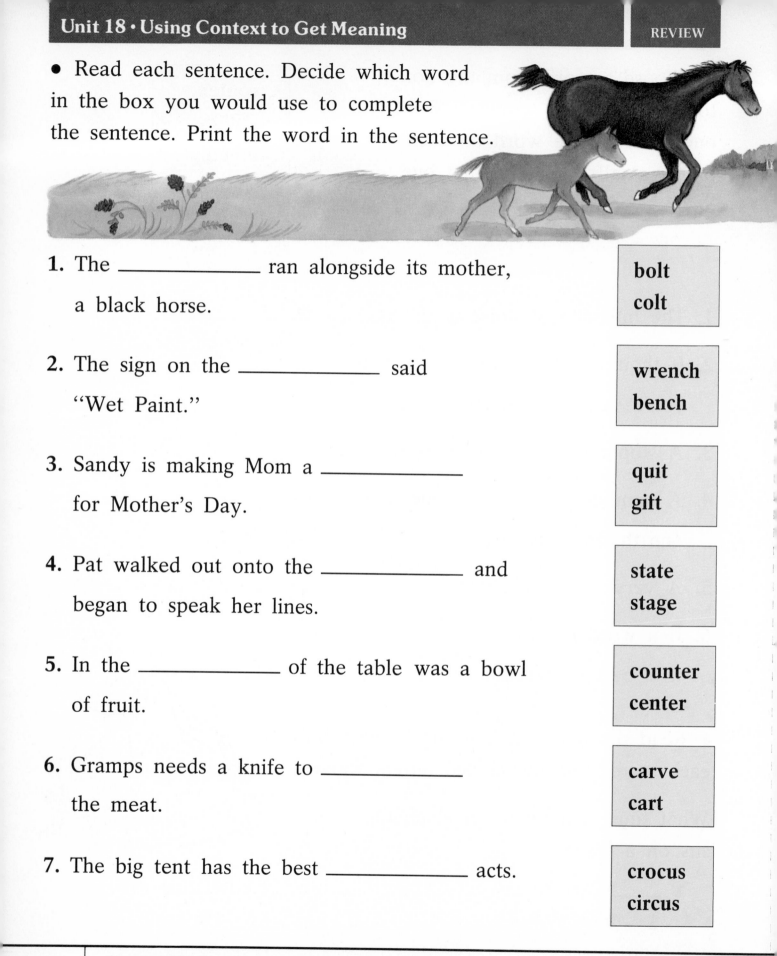

● Read each sentence. Decide which word in the box you would use to complete the sentence. Print the word in the sentence.

1. The _____ ran alongside its mother, a black horse.

bolt
colt

2. The sign on the _____ said "Wet Paint."

wrench
bench

3. Sandy is making Mom a _____ for Mother's Day.

quit
gift

4. Pat walked out onto the _____ and began to speak her lines.

state
stage

5. In the _____ of the table was a bowl of fruit.

counter
center

6. Gramps needs a knife to _____ the meat.

carve
cart

7. The big tent has the best _____ acts.

crocus
circus

● Read the numbered sentence. Then read the two sentences below. Underline the sentence that is true.

1. Ann, my best friend, gave this bracelet to me.
   a. Someone is talking to Ann.
   b. Ann is my best friend.

2. Princess, the pet goat, ate all the flowers.
   a. A goat ate the flowers.
   b. Someone is talking to a princess.

3. Mr. Lynn, the principal, gave a talk in the library.
   a. Mr. Lynn is the principal.
   b. Someone is talking to Mr. Lynn.

4. Spot, a cute little dog, is loved by his neighbors.
   a. Someone is talking to a dog.
   b. Spot is a cute little dog.

5. Captain White, an astronaut, has walked in space.
   a. Captain White is an astronaut.
   b. Someone is talking to Captain White.

6. Alma, my little sister, likes to play baseball.
   a. Alma is my sister.
   b. Someone is talking to Alma.

7. Mr. Jay, our teacher, told us a funny story.
   a. Someone is talking to Mr. Jay.
   b. Mr. Jay is our teacher.

8. Mr. Davis, the storeowner, always gives us fruit.
   a. Mr. Davis owns a store.
   b. Someone is talking to Mr. Davis.

Comprehension: Commas of Apposition

DISCOVERIES

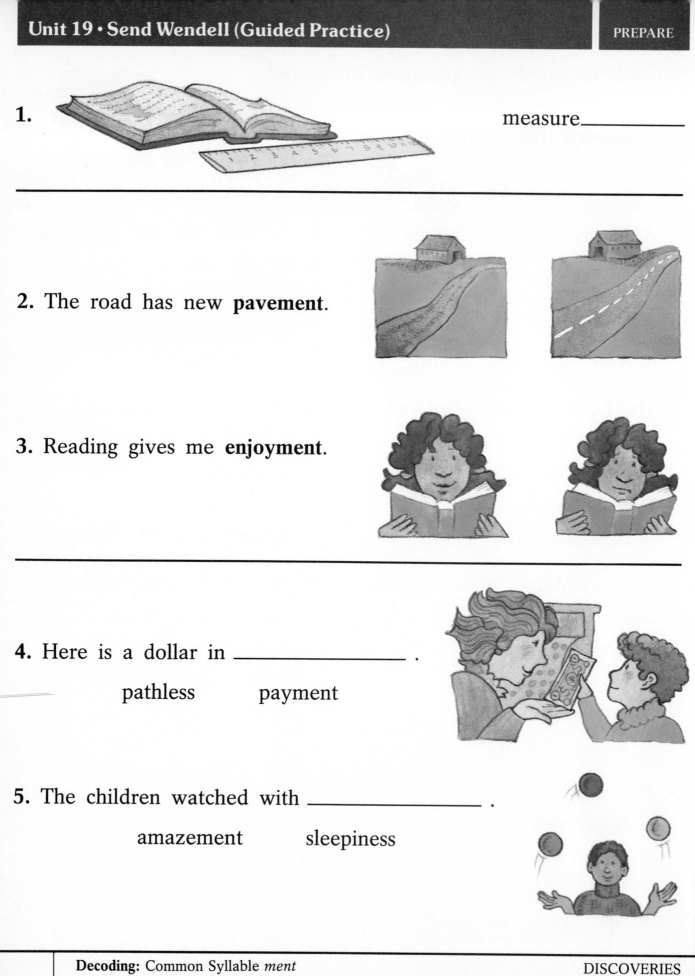

1. measure_____

2. The road has new **pavement**.

3. Reading gives me **enjoyment**.

4. Here is a dollar in _____.

   pathless   payment

5. The children watched with _____.

   amazement   sleepiness

• Circle the word that makes sense in each sentence. For the last one, mark the space for the answer.

1. On rainy days, we enjoy the playroom in our _____ .

     basement　　　blackness　　　casement

2. That _____ of goods arrived by truck.

     sharpness　　　shipment　　　seedless

3. Henry didn't like the _____ of the pictures on the wall.

     placement　　　priceless　　　payment

4. You can buy all kinds of things in a _____ store.

     department　　treatment　　　deepness

5. Finding the treasure caused a lot of _____ .

     emptiness　　　endless　　　　excitement

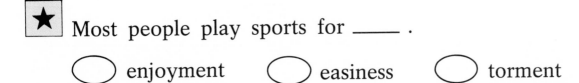

★ Most people play sports for _____ .

　　◯ enjoyment　　◯ easiness　　◯ torment

Decoding: Common Syllable *ment*

● Read each sentence and the words below it. Circle the word that belongs in the sentence. Then print that word in the sentence.

1. This baby is my _____.

    cousin   crayon   context

2. The baby's father is my _____.

    until   ugly   uncle

3. When I picked the baby up, he _____.

    gobbled   grazed   gurgled

4. I am _____ that the baby likes me!

    circle   certain   center

● Choose someone in your family to tell about. You might choose a favorite uncle or a cousin. Print sentences that tell about that person on the lines below.

_____

_____

_____

_____

• Think about "Send Wendell."
Read each question. Print the answer.
The page number tells where to look.

1. What did William and Alice always say when
   there was a job to be done? (page 230)

   _____

2. Who was coming to visit Wendell's family? (page 232)

   _____

3. Which child did the most to get ready for the visit? (page 232)

   _____

4. What was Wendell doing when his uncle came? (page 234)

   _____

5. Why did his uncle call Wendell a good boy? (page 234)

   _____

6. What did Uncle Robert invite Wendell to do? (page 238)

   _____

7. How did Wendell get his sister to help out? (page 238)

   _____

● Read each story and the questions on the right. Put an **X** by the answers to the questions.

Betty opened her umbrella when it started to rain. She carried it over her head, but she was still getting wet. "Rain must be coming in one side," she thought. So she carried her umbrella to one side. That didn't help. Then Betty looked at the umbrella and quickly found the problem. The umbrella had three big holes in it.

Why was Betty's umbrella open?

_____ The sun was shining.

_____ It had started to rain.

_____ The umbrella didn't work.

What happened because holes were in Betty's umbrella?

_____ She got lost.

_____ She didn't get wet.

_____ She got wet.

Tommy saw just the game he wanted. He picked it up and carried it to the front of the store. "I'll take it," he said to the man. He reached in his pocket for some money. Tommy got quite a surprise. He did not find coins. He found nothing but a big hole. The coins were gone. Tommy left the store without the game.

Why did Tommy need money?

_____ He wanted to buy a game.

_____ He wanted a new pocket.

_____ He wanted to buy a bird.

What happened because a hole was in Tommy's pocket?

_____ He could buy the game.

_____ He bought something else.

_____ His money fell out.

Comprehension: Understanding Cause-Effect Relationships

DISCOVERIES

Houghton Mifflin Reading, 1989 Edition

1
- ◯ trade
- ◯ trip
- ◯ test

- ◯ uncle
- ◯ animal
- ◯ until

- ◯ island
- ◯ idea
- ◯ inch

- ◯ spot
- ◯ spell
- ◯ speak

2
- ◯ wagon
- ◯ wash
- ◯ wide

- ◯ strange
- ◯ strong
- ◯ stood

- ◯ example
- ◯ excite
- ◯ eggs

- ◯ mountain
- ◯ moment
- ◯ means

3
- ◯ dress
- ◯ during
- ◯ dancing

- ◯ fact
- ◯ free
- ◯ fresh

- ◯ horses
- ◯ heavy
- ◯ heard

- ◯ drop
- ◯ dry
- ◯ deep

4
- ◯ east
- ◯ explain
- ◯ engine

- ◯ voice
- ◯ high
- ◯ ice

- ◯ million
- ◯ minute
- ◯ middle

- ◯ record
- ◯ reach
- ◯ rule

5
- ◯ basket
- ◯ brought
- ◯ build

- ◯ wagon
- ◯ against
- ◯ among

- ◯ captain
- ◯ certain
- ◯ center

- ◯ snake
- ◯ shape
- ◯ solve

Vocabulary Test
Find number 1. Look at the words in the first box. Find the word *trip*. Mark the space for the word. (Continue in this manner, pronouncing the words to be tested.)

DISCOVERIES

Houghton Mifflin Reading, 1989 Edition

1. Judy Small put on her coat.
She drove her car to work.

_____ Judy Small put on her coat.

_____ She drove her car to work.

2. Petunia woke up. She was hungry.
She went to drink some milk
from a plate. Then she purred softly.

3. This is Joey's favorite place.
He likes to walk on the warm sand.
He likes to jump in the waves. He
gives a little piece of his sandwich
to the seagulls.

_____ Joey is at the beach.

_____ Joey is in the woods.

_____ Joey is at the zoo.

Comprehension: Drawing Conclusions

Houghton Mifflin Reading, 1989 Edition

• Read each story and its question on the right. Underline the words that answer each question. For the last one, mark the space for the answer. Then underline the words in each story that helped you decide.

1. Alma came to a green fence. She didn't see the sign on it. So she leaned on the fence to rest. When she stood up, her dress was green!

What did the sign say?

DON'T WALK ON THE GRASS
PAINT FOR SALE
WET PAINT

2. Mr. Hill's cat had six kittens. He didn't know what to do with all the kittens. Then he put a sign on his door. Soon all the kittens were gone.

What did the sign say?

ANIMAL DOCTOR
FREE KITTENS
KEEP OUT!

3. David and his sister Mary were walking to school. Then Mary ran in front of David to the street. David called, "Stop now! Read the sign."

What did the sign say?

DON'T WALK
NO PARKING
FRESH FRUIT FOR SALE

★ Ben wanted to feed bread to the ducks at the pond. So he read the sign by the pond. Then Ben ate the bread himself.

What did the sign say?

◯ DUCKS FOR SALE
◯ DON'T FEED DUCKS
◯ FEED THE ANIMALS

Comprehension: Drawing Conclusions

DISCOVERIES

● Read each pair of words. Then read
the sentence to the right. Decide which
word makes sense in the sentence.
Print that word in the sentence.

1. joined   That make-believe story is

   giant   about a _____ .

2. police   A detective showed the class

   promise   around the _____ station.

3. roared   The lion _____ and whirled

   road   around in the ring.

4. terrible   You may lose your _____ ,

   temper   but don't throw tantrums.

5. elephant   During an _____ , you can

   earthquake feel the ground shake.

6. dinner   We could hear a train whistle far

   distance   in the _____ .

Vocabulary: "The Giant Who Threw Tantrums"

DISCOVERIES

Houghton Mifflin Reading, 1989 Edition

● Think about "The Giant Who Threw Tantrums."
Read each question. Print the answer.

1. Where did the giant live?

_____

_____

2. Why did the giant throw tantrums?

_____

_____

3. How did the villagers explain trees being
   knocked down and rocks bouncing?

_____

_____

4. How did the boy get the giant to stop
   throwing tantrums?

_____

_____

5. How did the police chief explain the long,
   low whistle sometimes heard in the distance?

_____

6. What do you think the whistle was?

_____

● Read each sentence and the words below it.
Circle the word that belongs in the sentence.
Then print that word in the sentence.

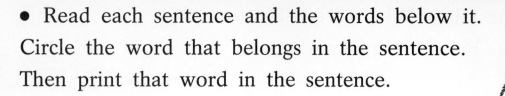

1. Jimmy's _____ tooth will fall out soon.

   loose   broom   moose

2. The glasses fell to the floor with a _____ .

   fresh   crash   eyelash

3. "I need to _____ because I'm late!" said the king.

   rush   hush   brush

4. The children _____ up when they heard the bell.

   brook   stood   shook

5. Ted won a prize for his turnips at the _____ .

   hairy   stairway   fair

6. The baby pigs sleep on a bed of _____ .

   straw   strainer   strikes

● Read the paragraph and follow the directions.

Mr. Wilson is working
on the new telephone books.
He is adding the names
of all the new people
in town. You can help him
by listing the names below
in alphabetical order.

Gipson	Gray	Goodman	Gardener
Frank	Fuller	Glass	Gerson
Folger	Henson	Hart	Hunter

1. _____   7. _____

2. _____   8. _____

3. _____   9. _____

4. _____   10. _____

5. _____   11. _____

6. _____   12. _____

Decoding: Alphabetical Order — 2nd Letter

• Read the paragraph and follow the directions.

Jimmy is putting together a book of animals. He has found pictures of many different kinds of animals. Help him by listing each group of animal names in alphabetical order.

giraffe	goat
fox	goldfish
goose	frog

pollywog	mouse
mole	monkey
pig	moose

1. _____

2. _____

3. _____

4. _____

5. _____

6. _____

1. _____

2. _____

3. _____

4. _____

5. _____

6. _____

★ Read the words. Find the word that comes first in alphabetical order. Mark the space for the answer.

◯ rain   ◯ radish   ◯ raccoon

● Read the words in the box.
Use them to complete the story.
Print one word on each line.

celebrate	grazing	areas
exciting	million	enjoy
mountains	islands	country

Japan is a beautiful _____ . Japan is made up of many small _____ . _____ cover most of the country. There are few _____ that are good for growing crops or _____ animals. Still, some farming is done. Many farmers grow rice. The people of Japan also farm the sea. They _____ eating seaweeds of all kinds — as well as lots of fresh fish.

Most of the people of Japan live in cities. These cities are _____ to visit. They are also crowded, for there are more than 116 _____ people in the tiny country. Most city people dress as we do. But on special days, some people _____ by wearing the lovely costumes of Japan's past.

● Read each sentence. Decide which of the words in the box you would use to complete the sentence. Print that word in the sentence.

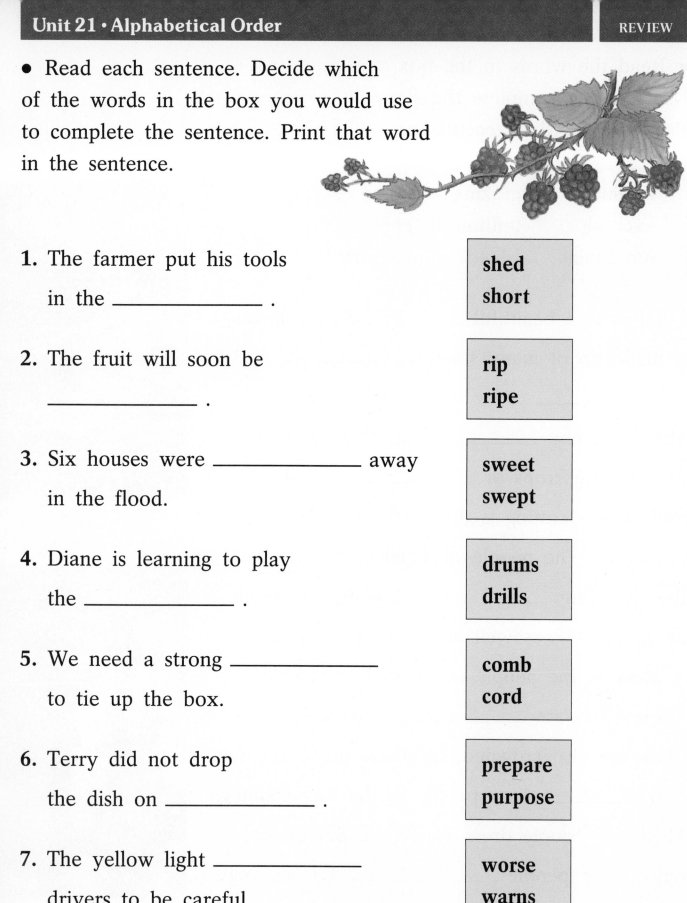

1. The farmer put his tools in the _____ .

shed
short

2. The fruit will soon be _____ .

rip
ripe

3. Six houses were _____ away in the flood.

sweet
swept

4. Diane is learning to play the _____ .

drums
drills

5. We need a strong _____ to tie up the box.

comb
cord

6. Terry did not drop the dish on _____ .

prepare
purpose

7. The yellow light _____ drivers to be careful.

worse
warns

Decoding/Phonics: Vowel Review — Short, Long, and Vowel plus *r*

DISCOVERIES

Houghton Mifflin Reading, 1989 Edition

• Look at the words in each box.
Circle the common syllable in each word.
Then decide which word you would use
to complete the sentence. Print
that word in the sentence.

1.

| payment |
| basement |
| monument |

Meet me by the _____
in the park.

2.

| merriment |
| department |
| amazement |

My father is working part-time
in a _____ store.

3.

| equipment |
| encouragement |
| development |

The only _____ you need
is a baseball and a bat.

4.

| payment |
| basement |
| measurement |

To take that _____ ,
you need a ruler.

• Read each pair of sentences. Then read the word meanings to the right. On the line before each sentence, print the number of the best meaning for the word in heavy black letters.

_____ I like to ride the **train**.

_____ Don will **train** his dogs to sit.

1. a number of cars that move together
2. to teach

_____ I heard Mary's voice **trail** off just before she went to sleep.

_____ The **trail** led us through the woods.

1. get softer and softer
2. path

_____ My dog likes to **roll** in the grass.

_____ I cannot eat one more **roll**.

1. kind of bread
2. turn over and over

_____ Draw a long **line** across the paper.

_____ Nick read the last **line** of the story.

1. row of words
2. long, thin mark

_____ I gave Clara a **present** for her birthday.

_____ Was Nate **present** at the meeting?

1. a gift
2. to be at a place

_____ We have new **tires** on the car.

_____ The baby **tires** early in the evening.

1. parts of wheels
2. becomes sleepy

Comprehension: Using Context to Get Meaning

DISCOVERIES

Houghton Mifflin Reading, 1989 Edition

1. Bea's coat is **pocketless.**

2. I need to **rebuild** it!

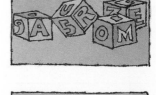

3. The boys **exchange** books.

4. Dad is in the **basement.**

5. The land around your house is your _____ .

   playful   property

6. Do you think that boat will stay _____ ?

   flatness   afloat

7. The children tried to _____ the lost cat.

   befriend   friendly

● Each word in the box begins or ends with a common syllable. Circle the letter or letters that make up the common syllable in each word.

afire	exact	wildly	basement
renew	beware	thankful	loudness
aloud	careless	motion	thirty

● Underline the word you would use to complete each sentence. For the last one, mark the space for the answer.

1. The sign told us to ____ of the dog.
　　aware　　　　beware　　　　warily

2. The ____ of its barking surprised me!
　　loudly　　　　aloud　　　　loudness

3. To be ____ , the dog weighs 7½ pounds.
　　action　　　　react　　　　exact

4. The dog has been ____ renamed Tiger.
　　renew　　　　newly　　　　newness

★ The dog's tail is always in ____ !
　　◯ motion　　◯ remove　　◯ moment

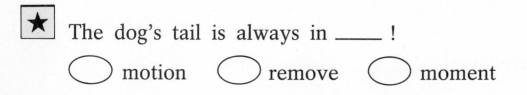

Decoding: Common Syllables

DISCOVERIES

Houghton Mifflin Reading, 1989 Edition

● Read the words in the box.
Use them to complete the sentences.
Print one word on each line.

repair	screwdriver	radio
wrench	strength	folks

1. Some tools are a hammer, a _____ ,

   a saw, and a _____ .

2. These tools can be used to build and

   _____ things.

3. Some tools help you do things that you might not

   have the _____ to do by yourself.

4. People can share ideas with each other by TV,

   phone, or _____ .

5. That radio show always begins with a voice

   saying "Good evening, _____ !"

● Print a sentence to answer each question.
Do you like to listen to the radio?
What do you like to listen to best?

_____

_____

_____

● Think about "It's Not Fair!"
Read each question. Print the answer.

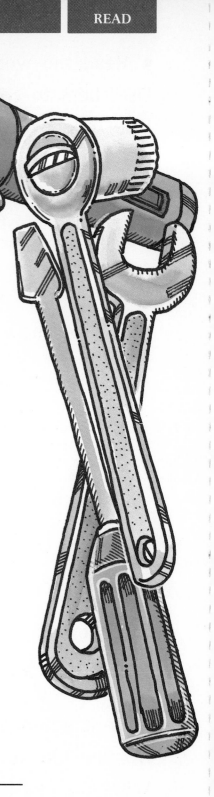

1. Who is telling this story?

_____

_____

2. Why doesn't Susan like being the oldest?
Give two reasons.

_____

_____

3. Who does Susan want to eat with?

_____

_____

4. What does Susan help her grandfather do?

_____

_____

5. What does Susan get to do after she helps her
grandfather?

_____

_____

6. How does that make her feel?

_____

Comprehension: "It's Not Fair"   DISCOVERIES

Houghton Mifflin Reading, 1989 Edition

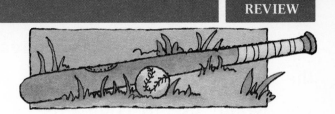

• Read each story.
Then follow the directions below.

Catherine Crocodile jumped off the school bus. She ran into the house. Quickly, she made a sandwich and ate it.

Then Catherine got her bat and ball. She ran outside. Catherine played two games of baseball with her friends.

Catherine ran home again. She watched a TV show. She ate supper. Then she played dominoes. After that, she did her homework.

Catherine Crocodile had a very busy evening!

1. What is the story's topic? Underline the answer.
   a. playing games
   b. friends
   c. Catherine Crocodile
2. Underline the sentence in the story that tells the main idea.

Harvey is late for everything. He is always the last to come to breakfast. By the time he sits down to eat, his eggs are cold.

Often, Harvey misses the bus to school. He has to ride his bike, so he is late for school.

Once, Harvey's friend Max decided to surprise Harvey. It was Harvey's birthday. Friends were at Max's house waiting. But Harvey was very, very late. When he got there, everyone had gone. Max was so angry he never told about the surprise.

1. What is the story's topic? Underline the answer.
   a. a birthday
   b. Harvey
   c. Max
2. Underline the sentence in the story that tells the main idea.

Comprehension: Getting the Topic/Main Idea   DISCOVERIES

● Read each sentence. Then read the answer choices. Circle the word you would use to complete the sentence.

1. Butter is made from ____ .

   croak   cream   creep

2. There is not much water in that ____ .

   broad   brook   broil

3. Try to ____ stepping in puddles.

   annoy   await   avoid

4. Listen to the ____ of the little chicks!

   plows   peeps   peaks

5. Do not ____ far from the house.

   stray   stream   straw

6. That runner needs to ____ speed.

   grief   gown   gain

7. Put this bread in the ____ .

   toaster   teaser   tailor

Decoding/Phonics: Vowel Pairs Review
Preintroduce the following new word that appears in the directions: *choices*.

DISCOVERIES

132

Houghton Mifflin Reading, 1989 Edition

1. Star, my horse, bolted from the barn. _____

2. We use books, pencils, and pens at school. _____

3. Please stand up now, Ramón. _____

_____

4. My favorite colors are red blue and yellow.

_____

_____

5. Eat your supper Freddy.

_____

_____

6. Mrs. Gold a firefighter showed us around the fire station.

7. Grandmother, did you know that Fang, my dog, likes cats, birds, and fish?

Comprehension: Commas in a Series, of Apposition, of Address   DISCOVERIES

Here are three reasons commas are used.

A. to show who is being spoken to

B. to separate a list of things

C. to tell more about someone or something that has just been named

● Read each sentence. Decide why commas were used. Print the letter of the reason next to each sentence.

_____ **1.** The box was filled with gold, bracelets, rings, and coins.

_____ **2.** Max, the neighbor's dog, just ate my shoe.

_____ **3.** Jed, will you help me with my homework?

_____ **4.** Mom, the elephant in the zoo just ran away.

_____ **5.** Dad's workbench was covered with hammers, nails, screwdrivers, and wrenches.

_____ **6.** Susan, the girl next door, loves to read.

★ Read the Sentence. How many things did Annie buy? Mark the space for the answer.

Annie went to the store to buy milk, corn bread, meat, and rice.

◯ 2   ◯ 3   ◯ 4

Comprehension: Commas in a Series, of Apposition, of Address

DISCOVERIES

Preintroduce the following new words that appear in the directions: *reasons, commas, spoken, separate.*

134

● Print words from the box under the
headings **urban area** and **rural area**.
Several words belong to both groups.

houses	museums	subways	farms
schools	country fairs	theaters	cornfields
stores	street fairs	apartments	hospitals

COMMUNITIES

urban area   rural area

_____   _____

_____   _____

_____   _____

_____   _____

_____   _____

_____   _____

_____   _____

● As you read "Communities — Large and Small,"
compare your answers with the information
in the article.

Vocabulary: "Communities — Large and Small"
Preintroduce the following new word that appears in the directions: *article*.

DISCOVERIES

Houghton Mifflin Reading, 1989 Edition

135

● Think about "Communities—Large and Small."
Look at each picture. Print **urban** or **rural**
under each picture.

_____   _____

● Print some sentences that tell about an urban area
or a rural area.

_____

_____

_____

_____

_____

_____

_____

● Read each sentence. Decide which of the words in the box you would use to complete the sentence. Print that word in the sentence.

1. The _____ ran much faster than the turtle.

| hire |
| hare |

2. The _____ is the inner part of some fruits.

| core |
| cure |

3. The _____ tire is in the back of the car.

| spire |
| spare |

4. We spent our summer vacation at the _____ .

| shone |
| shore |

5. Mr. Perkins may _____ you to rewrite that story.

| require |
| square |

6. Are you _____ of the danger of forest fires?

| aware |
| award |

7. A _____ of horns told us the parade was under way.

| blare |
| blur |

Decoding/Phonics: Vowel Plus re   DISCOVERIES

● Read each sentence. Then look at the word in heavy black letters. Circle the common syllable or syllables that have been added to the base word. Then write the base word. The first one has been done for you.

1. We were surprised at the **quickness** of the rabbit.

(ness)　　less　　___quick___

2. It seemed **senseless** to leave without seeing the museum.

ment　　less　　_____

3. There is nothing like the **freshness** of homemade bread.

ness　　ment　　_____

4. The **strangeness** of a new school made Sal feel frightened.

less　　ness　　_____

5. What is the **measurement** of that straight line?

ness　　ment　　_____

6. I thought the soup was **tasteless**, but I didn't say so.

ness　　less　　_____

7. After waiting so long for the train, we became **restless**.

less　　ment　　_____

8. A party is a time for laughter and **merriment**.

ness　　ment　　_____

Decoding: Common Syllables *less, ness, ment*

DISCOVERIES

Houghton Mifflin Reading, 1989 Edition

● Use the information in the box to make
a summary of the story "The Little Red Hen."
Print your summary on the lines below.

> **Main Character** = Little Red Hen
>
> **Setting** = field of wheat
>
> **First Event** = The hen finds some wheat,
> but none of her friends will help plant it.
>
> **Second Event** = The hen has to do all the work
> needed to make bread by herself.
>
> **Third Event** = When it's time to eat the bread,
> the hen decides not to share it
> with her lazy friends.

_____

_____

_____

_____

_____

_____

_____

_____

_____

● Read each sentence and the words below it.
Circle the word that belongs in the sentence.
Then print that word in the sentence.

1. Grandma made a warm _____ for my bed.

    queen   quiet   quilt

2. Alex _____ a wooden doll in crafts class.

    carved   crashed   career

3. Did you _____ my new cowboy hat?

    nothing   notice   noise

4. Mountain streams feed the river in the _____ .

    vowel   violin   valley

5. Ted used the old _____ for slippers.

    microphones   monsters   moccasins

6. It is _____ to sleep standing up!

    direction   difficult   delicious

7. Maria _____ to her cousin's letter.

    retired   repaired   replied

● Think about "Daniel's Duck."
Read each group of sentences.
The first sentence tells something that happened.
Underline the sentence below it that tells **why.**

1. Daniel's father gave him wood and a knife.
   a. Daniel wanted to help get dinner ready.
   b. Daniel wanted to carve an animal.

2. Jeff didn't think the duck was carved right.
   a. Its head was on backwards.
   b. The duck didn't have any wings.

3. Daniel decided to throw his duck in the river.
   a. People had laughed at the duck.
   b. No one wanted to buy the duck.

4. Henry Pettigrew had laughed at the duck, too.
   a. Daniel's duck made him feel happy.
   b. He thought Daniel's duck was ugly.

5. Daniel decided that his duck was not ugly.
   a. Mr. Pettigrew had said that it was good.
   b. Jeff had said that it was good.

6. Daniel wouldn't sell his duck to Mr. Pettigrew.
   a. He wanted to keep the duck for himself.
   b. He wanted to give the duck to Mr. Pettigrew.

Comprehension: "Daniel's Duck"

● Read the first sentence in each group. Then put an **X** before the sentence that is true.

1. For lunch we had fruit, cheese sandwiches, and carrots.

_____ We had three things for lunch.

_____ We had four things for lunch.

2. Doctor Davis, the baby has a terrible cold.

_____ Someone is talking to Doctor Davis.

_____ Doctor Davis has a bad cold.

3. Mr. Farr, the bus driver, likes to hear us sing.

_____ Mr. Farr is a bus driver.

_____ Someone is talking to Mr. Farr.

4. Mrs. Cook, my mother's best friend, drives us to school.

_____ Mrs. Cook is my mother's best friend.

_____ Someone is talking to Mrs. Cook.

5. When school starts I'll need pencils, paper, books, and a lunch box.

_____ I'll need three different things.

_____ I'll need four different things.

● Put the words in each group
in alphabetical order. Number
the words from **1** to **5** to show
the correct order.

1.

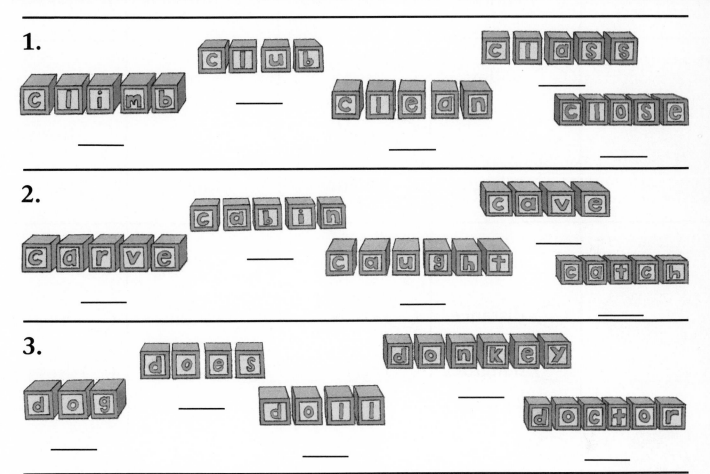

2.

3.

● Now print all the words
in alphabetical order.

1. _____ 6. _____ 11. _____

2. _____ 7. _____ 12. _____

3. _____ 8. _____ 13. _____

4. _____ 9. _____ 14. _____

5. _____ 10. _____ 15. _____

1

- ○ close
- ○ class
- ○ choose

- ○ meat
- ○ moon
- ○ moment

- ○ nothing
- ○ noise
- ○ notice

- ○ art
- ○ area
- ○ air

2

- ○ valley
- ○ voice
- ○ village

- ○ cook
- ○ cool
- ○ color

- ○ farm
- ○ fact
- ○ fair

- ○ thin
- ○ third
- ○ trip

3

- ○ during
- ○ distance
- ○ daughter

- ○ temper
- ○ trade
- ○ test

- ○ million
- ○ middle
- ○ material

- ○ dish
- ○ deep
- ○ dress

4

- ○ wing
- ○ wide
- ○ wash

- ○ shape
- ○ star
- ○ sharp

- ○ reach
- ○ reason
- ○ record

- ○ inch
- ○ ice
- ○ island

5

- ○ bag
- ○ bad
- ○ bit

- ○ east
- ○ explain
- ○ engine

- ○ bright
- ○ basket
- ○ build

- ○ solve
- ○ speak
- ○ snake

Vocabulary Test
Find number 1. Look at the words in the first box. Find the word *center*. Mark the space for the word. (Continue in this manner, pronouncing the words to be tested.)

DISCOVERIES

144

Houghton Mifflin Reading, 1989 Edition

A Bundle of Sticks

Characters

Old Man

Mina, his daughter

Amir, his son

Sudi, his daughter

Princess of Persia

Vizier, a high officer
at the palace

Princess: Your rug will make a fine present for the Prince. The prize is yours!

(Mina, Amir, Sudi, and the Old Man bow as the Princess and the Vizier leave.)

Mina and Amir: We won, Father! Thank you!

Sudi: We won, thanks to you, Father — and to your bundle of sticks!

Scene One

In the rug shop

Old Man: My rugs are the most beautiful in Persia, but I am getting old. I have worked hard all my life. Now I just want to sit in my garden. *(He calls out.)* Mina! Amir! Sudi!

Mina, Amir, Sudi *(Running into the shop):* What is it, Father?

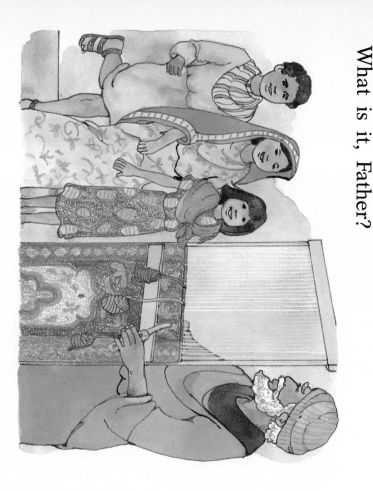

Mina *(Bowing):* We all did, Princess.

Princess: You *all* did? That is a surprise. You must work very well together. What is your secret?

Mina: It is no secret, Princess. You see, we have a bundle of sticks on our wall.

Princess: How strange! What has a bundle of sticks to do with working together?

Amir: It reminds us that alone each of us is weak, but that together we are strong.

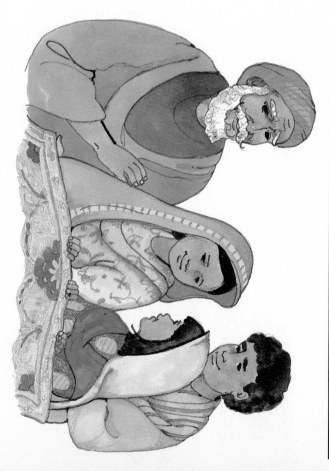

15

Old Man: I have something important to talk to you about. My children, it is time for me to retire and turn my shop over to you.

Mina: But, Father, no one in Persia makes finer rugs than you! How can we manage the shop without you?

Old Man: I have taught you all that I know, and you have learned your lessons well. Mina, your patterns are beautiful. They are as fine as my own.

Mina: Thank you, Father. You have taught me well. (*She sits and begins to draw.*)

Old Man: Amir, your dyes are bright and strong. You mix colors as well as I do.

Amir: Thank you, Father. You have taught me well. (*He sits and begins putting yarn into a pot of dye.*)

Scene Four
At the palace

(*Mina*, *Amir*, *and* *Sudi* *roll out a rug.* The *Old Man* *looks on.*)

Mina: Amir, look how your colors sparkle!

Amir: Sudi's weaving is better than ever!

Sudi: Mina's pattern is the finest ever!

Princess (*Arriving with the* ***Vizier***): This rug is beautiful! Which of you made it?

Old Man: Sudi, your weaving is smooth and even. You work the loom as well as I do.

Sudi: Thank you, Father. You have taught me well. (*She sits down at the loom.*)

Old Man: Remember, my children, that the finest rugs in Persia are made in this shop. Work well together, and you will have no problems.

Old Man (*Taking the bundle*): It is easy to break one stick. It is more difficult to break a bundle. Do you understand?

Mina: Yes, Father. I think we do. Alone, we are weak, as were the sticks.

Amir: But together we are strong, as is the bundle of sticks.

Sudi: You have taught us well, Father.

Old Man (*Hanging the bundle of sticks up on the wall*): Now back to work with you! Time is short. There is much to be done if you are to win the prize.

Scene Two
At the palace

Vizier (*Coming into the room*): You called, Princess?

Princess: Yes, yes. I am troubled.

Vizier: Troubled? But, Princess, why are you troubled?

Princess (*Walking up and down*): I am going to visit the Prince of Bagdad. I want to give him a present, but I can think of nothing fine enough.

Mina (*Groaning*): I cannot do it, Father.

Amir: Let me try. (*He takes the bundle but is unable to break it.*) I can't do it. You try, Sudi. (*He gives the bundle to Sudi.*)

Sudi (*Groaning*): It can't be done, Father!

Houghton Mifflin Reading, 1989 Edition

Vizier: Oh, that is very troubling, indeed. (*He, too, walks up and down, thinking. He stops suddenly.*) Why not give the Prince a rug? All the world knows Persia for its beautiful rugs.

Princess (*Sitting down*): Of course! Order the rug makers of Persia to get to work. Tell them to bring their finest rugs here in one month. I will choose the most beautiful rug. The rug maker will have a grand prize!

Vizier: I will spread the news at once.

Old Man: (*Racing into the shop*): Look what you have done! I thought I had taught you well, but I see that it's time for one more lesson. Go outside, now, all of you. Bring me some sticks. Go quickly!

(***Mina, Amir,*** *and* ***Sudi*** *run out of the shop. The* ***Old Man*** *pulls the dye table to the front of the shop. After a while, his children return with four sticks each.*)

Old Man: Each of you keep one stick. Give me the rest. (*He takes three sticks from each and places them on the table.*) Can you break the stick you are holding?

Mina: Of course, Father. (*She breaks a stick.*)

Amir (*Breaking a stick*): It's easy, Father.

Sudi (*Breaking a stick*): It's nothing, Father. (*The* ***Old Man*** *ties the sticks on the table into a bundle. He hands it to* ***Mina.***)

Old Man: Now break this bundle of sticks.

Scene Three
In the rug shop

Mina: Amir! Sudi! Did you hear the news? Did you hear about the prize?

Amir: Yes, we did. Isn't it exciting?

Sudi: If we win, we will be famous. Everyone in Persia will buy our rugs!

Mina: We must get right to work. Already I've started to plan the pattern.

Sudi (*Shouting*): Well, I happen to think I'm the most important one. There can be no rug if I do not weave it. By right, I should have the prize.

Mina (*Tearing up her drawing*): See if you can make a rug without my pattern!

Amir (*Knocking the dye pots to the floor*): Try to make a rug without my dyes!

Sudi (*Knocking over the loom*): See how far you can get without my weaving!

Houghton Mifflin Reading, 1989 Edition

Amir: I must start mixing my dyes. (*He hurries to his table and begins mixing.*)

Sudi: And I must make sure my loom is ready. (**Amir and Sudi** *do not notice as* **Mina** *rises and goes to the window to get a better look at her drawing.*)

Mina (*Whispering*): This pattern is good. It is sure to delight the Princess. How nice it would be if I alone won the prize. After all, the pattern is the most important part of rug making.

Sudi (*Looking up at Mina*): Show us the pattern, Mina. We want to see it!

Mina: No! I have worked hard, and this is the best pattern I have ever made. I don't think I should have to share the prize. After all, without my pattern, where would you two be?

Amir (*Angrily*): Where indeed! Would there be a rug at all without my colors? Maybe I alone should have the prize.

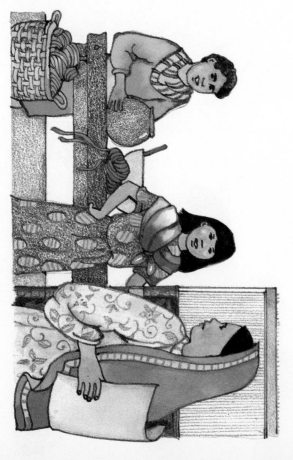